POEMS *of* COLOR

Knitting in the Bohus Tradition

WENDY KEELE

INTERWEAVE PRESS

To Emma Jacobsson

and the designers and knitters of Bohus Stickning.

Design, Susan Wasinger, Signorella Graphic Arts
Photography, Joe Coca
Illustration, Susan Strawn
Production, Marc McCoy Owens
Technical editing, Dorothy T. Ratigan

 Interweave Press, Inc.
201 East Fourth Street
Loveland, Colorado 80537
USA

Printed in Hong Kong by Sing Cheong

Library of Congress Cataloging-in-Publication Data

Keele, Wendy, 1959–
    Poems of color : knitting in the Bohus tradition / Wendy Keele.
        p.   cm.
    Includes index.
    ISBN 1-883010-12-8
    1. Knitting—Sweden—Bohuslän—History—20th century.   2. Bohus
Stickning—History.   I. Title.
    TT819.S82B645   1995
    746.43'2'09486—dc20   95-30581
                                                           CIP

First printing: IWP—7.5M:895:CC
Second printing: IWP—7.5M:396:CC

PREFACE

I am often asked how I became interested in Bohus Stickning. Am I of Swedish descent or do I speak the language? Unfortunately, the answer is "no" on both counts. The saga started in September of 1986 when my mother and I traveled from Nebraska to Minneapolis, Minnesota, to attend a knitter's weekend called "Knitter's Days". At the time, I was "at home" with our two sons, ages two years and three months, and spent my afternoons dreamily thinking of knitting and designing. So a weekend of knitting sounded both relaxing and exciting. It was at Knitter's Days that I first saw a Bohus Stickning sweater. It was a moth-eaten, neglected example of Anna-Lisa Mannheimer Lunn's "The Red Edge". But even in its deplorable condition, the sweater was so different from any design I'd ever seen that I was intrigued.

That began my nine-year quest to learn more about Bohus Stickning and to write this book. It has included countless hours of researching, writing, knitting, and three trips to Sweden. There have been times of great frustration but even more times of overwhelming joy. The opportunity to write this book has been a wonderful blessing.

ACKNOWLEDGEMENTS

My greatest appreciation goes to Ingrid Mesterton for permission to publish the Bohus Stickning patterns. She opened her home, her mother's beloved business, and her heart to me. Thanks also go to Gunne Jacobsson for making my mother and me feel at home in Sweden.

I will always be grateful to the Bohus Stickning designers: Kerstin Olsson, Karin Ivarsson, and Annika Malmström-Bladini for taking the time to recollect their experiences as designers for Bohus Stickning. Kerstin also spent hours helping me identify patterns and she provided me with original pattern graphs, photographs, knitting swatches, and arranged the garments for photography.

I'd also like to thank Marianne Erikson, textiles curator at the Röhss Museum of Arts and Crafts; Ulla Häglund, textiles curator at The City of Gothenburg Museum; and Marie Johansson, curator at the Bohusläns Museum, for their assistance in my research.

To my knittingest friend, Joan Schrouder, special thanks go for her enthusiasm, technical knitting advice, knitting talents, and for introducing me to Karen Vanderpool, Kathy Juhlin, and Eugene Beugler. These four knitters gave generously of their talents and helped construct the garments for this book.

I'm deeply indebteded to Meg Swansen for her continual and unrelenting belief in this book and for introducing me to Jan Kimmet and her exquisite yarns. It was Jan's beautiful yarns and Mary Jo Burke's talents at dyeing that produced the yarns necessary for the angora-blend garments featured in this book.

I'm honored to have my book among the many fine books published by Interweave Press, and am grateful to Linda Ligon for seeing that possibility in my manuscript and to Deborah Cannarella for her help with its structure. My sincere respect and appreciation go to Judith Durant and Ann Budd for their careful editing and guidance through the many steps of this project. I am also grateful to Dot Ratigan for proofreading and editing the knitting instructions.

Last but not least, thanks go to the members of my family. To my mother, my first knitting teacher and traveling companion; my Dad, who I wish could see this "published" book; to Ben, Greg, Marcia, Alex, and Emma, the most wonderful children a mother could pray for, who understood the importance of this book and waited patiently countless times while "I just finish this row"; and finally to my husband John, who never wavered in his support and belief in this book and in me.

CONTENTS

INTRODUCTION

If a group of knitters were asked to name various knitting styles, they might list Fair Isle, gansey, and Shetland lace. However, few knitters would include Bohus knitting, a style of knitting that developed in southwestern Sweden in the province of Bohuslän. Most knitters are unfamiliar with Bohus knitting because the patterns have been well protected from reproduction. Only one Swedish book and a small number of magazine articles have ever featured Bohus knitting, and these did not include graphs of the color patterns. This is the first book to highlight the history of the organization, to introduce the designers and knitters, and to include graphs of original Bohus designs.

Knowledge of Bohus knitting is limited not because its history and patterns have been lost over time—the organization was in operation until 1969. What restricted the spread of information was the intentional decision to produce an exclusive product that was not reproduced outside of the organization.

Bohus Stickning was born out of one remarkable woman's attempt to provide relief work for local women during the depression in the 1930s and 1940s. Emma Jacobsson's primary objective was to find a product that women could produce at home while they cared for their families, one that they could sell to supplement their family's income. After much trial and error, the craft of hand knitting was selected. Initially, plain, utilitarian socks and mittens were produced. However, Emma soon realized that if the line of garments were expanded into the realm of fashion, higher prices could be commanded. Consequently, cardigan and pullover sweaters that had either knit-in designs or embroidered embellishments were made. These early garments were made from sport-weight natural-colored yarns.

Later, after World War II and economic recovery, Bohus Stickning expanded its line to include angora-blend yarns in a wide palette of stunning colors and array of garment styles and distributed its knitwear to the international market. Fewer of the knitters depended on their income to supplement their family's income, and more were women who simply wanted the opportunity to knit the beautiful designs. Likewise, Bohus Stickning's role changed from providing relief work for the women to an organization that developed and marketed fine knitwear designs internationally.

Emma was protective of the designs produced by Bohus Stickning and took measures to impede mass reproduction of them. She stipulated that the designs could not be reproduced until fifty years after her death. Meticulous business records, sample garments, graphs, and other business information were donated to local museums and archives.

But it was not Emma's intent to have her beloved Bohus Stickning designs forgotten. Therefore, Emma's daughter, Ingrid Mesterton, has granted special permission for the graphs to be included in this book. Every attempt has been made to preserve the integrity of the designs while updating the fit of the garments and using commercially available yarn.

Knitters of today will find inspiration in the beautiful designs, unusual color combinations, and subtle purl-stitch textures. In these patterns they will find a connection to the women who turned a cottage industry into an international business.

THE WOMEN OF BOHUS STICKNING AND THEIR ORGANIZATION

A sweater with a Bohus Stickning label is synonymous with a finely knit and designed garment. Knitwear for the Bohus Stickning organization was produced by highly skilled hand knitters from the province of Bohuslän in southwestern Sweden (the Swedes refer to this area as the province of Gothenburg and Bohus). For thirty years, this twentieth-century cottage industry flourished under the leadership of Emma Jacobsson. Bohus Stickning provided relief work and a modest supplemental income to women whose families were financially stressed by the depression in the 1930s. Initially, the knitters produced coarse, natural-color mittens and socks. But in time, Bohus Stickning transformed from products that were largely considered charity work to an exclusive art form. As the business developed, the variety of knitted garments increased to include cardigans, pullovers, tams, gloves, and scarves, all knit in fine multicolored angora-blend yarns. During its thirty-year life, Bohus Stickning produced more than 400 designs that were sold in Sweden and internationally.

Bohus Stickning was more than just a cottage industry and financial source for its workers. It served as an important social function for many of the knitters. With Emma Jacobsson as leader, designer, and businesswoman, Bohus Stickning evolved into a successful enterprise that produced truly unique and beautiful knitted designs. Emma selected five other talented females to help with the design process: Vera Bjurström, Anna-Lisa Mannheimer Lunn, Annika Malmström-Bladini, Kerstin Olsson, and Karin Ivarsson. Their designs were reproduced by hand by literally hundreds of skilled knitters throughout the province of Bohuslän. The vast majority of the knit-

The Bohus label was the sign of a high quality garment.

For thirty years, Bohus Stickning flourished under the leadership of Emma Jacobsson.
Photograph courtesy of Ingrid Mesterton.

ters were women though a few of the knitters' husbands and a few blind men also knit.

EMMA JACOBSSON

There were many women whose contributions to Bohus Stickning were important and influential; however, Emma Jacobsson's involvement was the key element that propelled the organization forward to success. Emma had not focused her goals in life on developing a cottage industry. Instead, a combination of her background, personality, and life opportunities directed her into leading the venture.

Emma Stiasny was born in 1883 in Vienna, Austria, the daughter of a respected Jewish glove maker. As a young adult, she chose to study fine arts in school and dreamed of being an artist. But being very self-critical, Emma felt that she would be unable to support herself by way of her artistic talents. Instead, she chose to explore her interest in nature and earned a Ph.D. in botany.

Emma was working at a botanical institute near Berlin when she met Malte Jacobsson, a Swedish student who was studying philosophy. The decision to marry Malte in 1912 was trying for Emma. It required her to leave her relatives, friends, and work and to move to Sweden, where Malte had been hired as a professor at Gothenburg University. It was a difficult transition, but as the years passed, Emma came to love Bohuslän. Ingrid Mesterton, Emma's daughter, said, "Here she felt at home. Wherever she was, her thoughts returned to the firm, polished cliffs of Bohus. In this province she experienced moments of extreme happiness."

It was not socially acceptable for Emma to continue her scientific career in Sweden—she was expected to focus on her new role as a wife. Instead, Emma turned to studying art history and published several papers about her research. In 1934, Malte became politically active and was elected governor of Bohuslän. Emma's research activities were replaced with her new duties as wife of the governor.

It was while Emma was the governor's wife that she realized one of her greatest challenges and successes. In 1937, a group of women came to Emma, asking her to help them start a home-based industry in response to the widespread depression in the 1930s. (The depression was particularly devastating for the families of stone cutters in the rural areas of the province where paving stones were cut for use in streets and sidewalks in Sweden and abroad. The development of asphalt as a new surfacing material and exportation problems to a politically troubled Germany lowered the demand for stone and led to high unemployment among stone cutters.) At the time, it was customary for women to stay at home caring for the family, home, and in some cases, the farm. The depression forced the women to search for ways to make money to help support their households. Although Emma did not feel qualified to lead the group, she was sympathetic to the women's needs, and decided to work with them in their experiments with different cottage industries. Ultimately, it was Emma's background in fine arts, her high standards, and her business sense that enabled her to help the women by establishing Bohus Stickning.

At first, the women made Christmas ornaments to sell at a Christmas market, splitting the proceeds among the participants. Although the ornaments sold well, the seasonal product did not provide year-round income. While searching for another profitable cottage industry, Emma and the women looked for the

Early Bohus Stickning patterns were for sturdy, plain, natural-colored socks and mittens that were sold at the Swedish Handicraft Store. Photograph courtesy of Ingrid Mesterton.

following three criteria:

1. A craft that could be produced on a continuous basis.

2. A craft that required no specialized equipment.

3. A craft that all the women could participate in.

With this in mind, the women next experimented with making stuffed animals. Emma asked a friend and skilled craftsperson, Vera Bjurström, to design stuffed animals and oversee their production. Vera's calico stuffed animals—donkeys, giraffes, and pigs—were charming and full of character. Unfortunately, Vera's talents for bringing character to the stuffed animals could not be reproduced by the other women, and though Vera delighted in designing the animals, she was not interested in leading their production.

Still determined to find a home-based industry, the women decided to try handknitting, a time-honored tradition throughout Sweden. Instead of following traditional Scandinavian designs, they wanted to use knitting designs that were locally derived. But unlike other areas of Sweden, Bohuslan did not have a regional knitting style. The women therefore decided to create their own designs. Emma's fine-arts training and knitting skills provided her with the tools to develop many of the first designs produced by Bohus Stickning. Vera also redirected her skills to create early Bohus Stickning designs.

The initial patterns were for socks and mittens. Sturdy, plain, natural-colored socks and mittens were sold at the Swedish Handicraft Store and ordered by the Gothenburg Street Administration and the Port Authority who oversaw street and harbor maintenance. Although the durable socks and mittens were pricey, they were ideal for keeping the street and harbor workers' feet and hands dry and warm. Encouraged by the success of the plain items and hoping to command a higher price for their product, the women began to knit with many colors and to

The governor's residence housed the Bohus Stickning headquarters from 1939 to 1950.

embellish their works with embroidery. Emma took samples of the embellished socks and mittens to several large, exclusive department stores in Stockholm. Much to her delight, several of the stores placed substantial orders. As a result, Emma was confident that a knitting cottage industry would provide a steady income for the women in the province. In 1940, Bohus Stickning expanded its line of products to include scarves, hats, pullover sweaters, and cardigans.

The Bohus Stickning organization was officially established on September 12, 1939, with a board of directors and Emma Jacobsson as the volunteer leader. On October 12, 1940, at the first meeting of the board of directors, the Purpose of Bohus Stickning was stated:

1. To stimulate the interest in knitting in the province of Bohuslän.

2. To keep those who knit within the province employed.

3. To help market the products.

Because Emma was the volunteer leader of Bohus Stickning, the organization was headquartered in the governor's residence in Gothenburg from 1939 to 1950. It was an opportune, rent-free location. The residence was conveniently located on a canal where boats could deliver huge quantities of raw wool from the wool producers. Bohus Stickning was accommodated in two rooms on the ground floor by the entrance. As the industry prospered, rooms adjacent to the kitchen were used for sorting wool and ironing garments. Visitors to the mansion were met at the entrance with the acid smell of wool, reminiscent of the old days when women were largely occupied with handspinning wool and cooking. When the royal family visited the governor's residence, yarns and garments were temporarily stowed away to transform one of the rooms into a dining room for the royal family's staff.

By 1950, Bohus Stickning was no longer viewed as relief work or a charity function within Sweden. The successful business, largely identified by finely knit, angora-blend sweaters with dazzling arrays of color, had expanded into the international market.

Bohus Stickning's function as a commercial business led to increased expenses. A need for more room, Malte Jacobbsson's retirement as governor, and the end of Emma and Malte's marriage in 1950 prompted Emma to find a new location for Bohus Stickning headquarters and added the price of rent to the already increasing operating costs. In addition, the expanding organization hired more staff members, the first paid designer, and paid Emma Jacobsson a modest salary.

The Gothenburg headquarters were moved to a new building with specially designed offices and features including a chute to the basement for wool deliveries, an elevator to transport wool stored in the basement to the workrooms upstairs, a thermohygrograph to record the temperature and humidity of the wool storage room, and a visitors' entrance used as a show room. The wool sorting and yarn storage rooms were located on the east side of the building. The yarn storage rooms were filled with the hundreds of colors of yarn available to the designers. (Seeing all the colors in the room must have been breathtaking. Unfortunately, no color photograph of the yarn room is available.) The south side contained the main office, showroom, and Emma's office. The designers' rooms and a pattern room containing a card catalog of yarn samples were located on the west side. Emma lived in a second-floor apartment in the same building.

Designer Kerstin Olsson was hired by Bohus Stickning in 1958. She is pictured here in the display room holding "The Chinese" designed by Emma. Photograph courtesy of Ingrid Mesterton.

Above: *Sketch of "The Snake" from Emma's sketchbook. The design was inspired by Peruvian textiles on display at the Gothenburg Ethnographic Museum.* Photograph courtesy of Ingrid Mesterton. Right: *After knitting countless swatches, "The Snake" was incorporated into a pullover sweater.* Courtesy of the City of Gothenburg Museum. Photo by Claes Jansson.

EMMA AS DESIGNER

Emma produced the majority of her designs during the early years of Bohus Stickning. At the time, the yarns used by Bohus Stickning were 100% sport- or worsted-weight wool in either natural or plant-dyed colors. Emma usually worked with two natural colors of wool to create motifs that were distinct and well defined. Many of Emma's designs were inspired by museum visits in Gothenburg and abroad. Her sketchbooks contain motifs that were influenced by displays at the Victoria and Albert Museum in London, as well as designs inspired by Peruvian weavings, Chinese ornaments, and a French art exhibit. She would make a sketch of the design and then knit countless swatches varying the motif size, yarn color, weight, and fiber content until she was satisfied with the overall effect. She then pinned the swatch to a natural-colored sweater (worked in stockinette stitch) to determine where the motifs should be knitted into a garment. The motifs were usually placed on the fronts of sweaters that had plain sleeves and backs. Directions for the proposed garment were then given to an expert knitter, who completed a prototype for Emma's review.

Emma was a perfectionist and was extraordinarily determined to achieve the results she desired. She spent one entire summer manipulating a carnation motif before she was pleased with the results. Creating a new pattern was a difficult process for Emma. Being so self-critical, she agonized over new designs. Emma likened the design process to childbirth, calling it "eine schwere Geburt", German for a difficult delivery.

Some of Emma's designs. Clockwise from top center, "The Woven Fabric", "The Flying Fence", "The Lamb", "The Goat", another version of "The Goat", "The Chinese", "The Turning Edge", and "The Lion". **Photograph courtesy of Ingrid Mesterton.**

EMMA AS COLLABORATOR

As the business aspects of Bohus Stickning grew, Emma had less time for designing. Instead, she focused her energies on directing Bohus Stickning and serving as an advisor and collaborator with the other five designers creating new patterns.

The designers were primarily responsible for producing new patterns that could be identified with the characteristic Bohus style established in the late 1940s—fine wool or angora-blend yarns, a wide palette of colors, and textural interest created by purl and garter stitches on a stockinette stitch background.

Their challenge was to make patterns that were new and different but consistent with the style of Bohus Stickning. The designers were encouraged to experiment with different types of yarn, colors, and patterns, with only the vague restriction that the yarn floats across the back of the garments could not get "too long". Their purpose wasn't just to make patterns that would sell, but to make beautiful patterns, each one more beautiful than the last.

Emma's involvement in design creation came after the designers knit narrow strips, or ribbons, of patterns. Emma would pin out the parts of the ribbons

In this 1943 photo, a model wears "The Slanting Square" designed by Vera Bjurström.
"The Lamb" on the left and "The Large Carnation" on the right were both designed by Emma.
The mittens are unidentified. Photograph courtesy of Ingrid Mesterton.

she did not like. By placing a small mirror on a "corrected" knitted ribbon, Emma evaluated if a mirror image of a motif was needed or if the motif should be repeated. The ribbon would be returned to the designer with a small note encouraging or discouraging continuation of the design. Emma's comments reflected her keen sense of design: "Too Boring"; "Onward! Not so small"; "Oh! Oh! Oh!"; "Too Much Color!—Moderation is good say the Greek". The designer would then knit a revised ribbon and submit it for further evaluation. This process continued until Emma approved the design. Once approved, the new design would be named and go into production.

EMMA THE BUSINESSWOMAN

An efficient and quality-oriented system of knitter education, garment production, correspondence, and payment was followed throughout the thirty-year operation of Bohus Stickning. Many changes in yarns, designs, and knitters took place, but the basic system remained intact. Emma insisted that her high standards be met in all phases of production, from sorting the raw wool, to teaching the knitters, to critiquing the finished products, to having mother-of-pearl buttons specially dyed to match the yarns. It was this tight control that enabled Bohus Stickning to maintain the high quality of its products.

The first step in the production of a Bohus Stickning garment began with selection of the best wool to be spun into yarn. Wool producers brought bags of raw wool to the Bohus Stickning headquarters where Emma and her wool expert sorted it according to length, thickness, curl, softness, transparency, and glossiness. The wool that did not meet Bohus Stickning standards was sold to one of the local wool mills that produced carpets, or it was returned to the pro-

ducer. Emma kept meticulous records, and each wool producer was given an invoice listing shipment date, weight of wool delivered, and weight of wool purchased. It was unusual for all of a producer's wool to be accepted by Bohus Stickning. Some producers tried only once to sell their wool to Bohus Stickning, a few producers consistently delivered quality wool. For example, of the 232.5 kg of fine wool delivered by M. Hultman from 1950–1952, 217.4 kg (93%) were purchased by Bohus Stickning. Fall wool was preferred to spring wool because it was of higher quality, cleaner, and therefore was easier to sort. As many as forty wool producers concurrently delivered wool to Bohus Stickning.

Wool producers were given a critique of each delivery: "Fine, good length, light, soft and glossy"; "Considerable decrease in quality since April"; "The management seems to be good except that the tips of the wool were sticking together and a little dry. The wool underneath was white and fine." Bohus Stickning demanded high-quality wool and paid higher prices than other buyers to entice producers to manage top-quality herds and deliver only the best wool.

After the wool was sorted, it was sent to one of a number of woolen mills to be spun into yarns specifically for Bohus Stickning. World War II was a difficult period for finding quality wool—Emma struggled with both wool producers and spinners to maintain the quality of yarn required for her garments.

Emma had contracted the Finnish textiles company, Domestic Wool, to spin a finer weight yarn than the Swedish wool spinners could produce. Unfortunately, the war forced greater restrictions on trade and business with foreign companies, and made it increasingly difficult to work with Domestic Wool. A special license was required from the Ministry of

*Bohus Stickning demanded high quality wool and paid higher prices
than other buyers. Emma and expert wool sorter, Signe Robertsson, examine a
shipment before sending it out to be spun. Photograph courtesy of Ingrid Mesterton.*

The first step in the production

of a Bohus Stickning garment began with selection

of the best wool to be spun into yarn.

Agriculture's Veterinary Department for Bohus Stickning's wool to be sent to Finland for spinning. Once when the license was refused, Emma solicited the Crown Prince of Sweden to persuade the Ministry of Agriculture to grant the license. On that occasion, permission was granted. However, as the war continued, no yarns were allowed to be shipped out of Finland, forcing Bohus Stickning to find mills within Sweden to spin the finer yarn they required.

Emma's desire for a yarn that was softer against the skin than fine wool led her to Greta Wahlman's angora mill. Emma and Greta corresponded and Emma thoroughly researched angora-blend yarns on her own—she even experimented with raising her own angora rabbits at a friend's house outside of town. As Emma reported to the Board of Directors in 1942, ". . . to make high-quality angora yarns, both angora and fine wool are needed. Mrs. Wahlman also informed me that the quality of the fine wool was very important for the quality of the final yarn. The wool must therefore be sorted very carefully so that only the finest, lightest, shiniest, and softest fibers are used. This sorting is essential for the high-quality angora yarn." Up to this time, angora yarns had never been spun in Sweden, but for Bohus Stickning, the Wahlman angora mill created a yarn of 70% fine wool and 30% angora. The Bohus Stickning staff aptly named the yarn Emma Jacobsson Angora (EJA).

During the 1950s, as the popularity of angora-blend garments increased, Emma searched for an even finer, softer angora yarn for Bohus Stickning. Because the wool mills in Sweden did not have the technology to spin a yarn with the high percentage of angora (50–70%) she desired, Emma looked for a foreign spinner. In 1956, she asked the Italian angora mill, Filatura di Chiavazza, to spin the fine wool and an-gora that she and her wool expert had hand sorted. Initially, the general manager insisted that they work only with Italian materials, but after Emma showed him her samples, he agreed to work with her high-quality materials.

Bohus Stickning worked closely with Filatura di Chiavazza to produce fine quality angora-blend yarns. Just as every detail of the business was closely monitored, strict attention was paid to yarn production. Emma and the Italian yarn spinner corresponded for more than two years about light brown spots that appeared on the 60% angora yarn. Bohus Stickning sent a hank of the spotted yarn to the spinner for his evaluation. Over the course of many letters, five possible explanations were given:

1. The spots were caused by the cardboard boxes within which the yarn was shipped.

2. The yarn needed to be washed before it was dyed.

3. The yarn was stored on metal shelves.

4. The spinning oil had oxidized.

5. The moth-proofing procedure caused the spots.

No satisfactory explanation for the spots was ever found.

During its thirty years of operation, Bohus Stickning supervised production of four types of yarn: Angora (50–60% angora, 40–50% wool), EJA (25–30% angora, 70–75% wool), Finewool (100% finger-weight wool) and Rya (100% worsted-weight wool). These specially spun yarns were used exclusively by Bohus Stickning. The organization also purchased two different types of pure wool yarn from Finland: Fin Wool and Q yarn. The Q yarn was a two-ply yarn, some of which had two different colors in the plies, similar to a ragg wool.

Along with Göta Trägårdh, a friend and design

teacher from Stockholm, Emma devoted considerable time to selecting colors for Bohus Stickning yarns. Acting as Bohus Stickning's color spy, Göta attended fashion shows in Paris where each year's new colors would be premiered. (The upcoming colors were kept secret and were not common knowledge.) Göta would scavenge snips of fabric, paper, netting, or ribbon in the new colors and send them to Emma. Emma, in turn, would take the color swatches to Bohus Stickning's master dyer, Gösta Juhlin. Working in his basement, Gösta would dye batch after batch of yarn until he achieved the exact color. The dye formula was then given to a commercial dyeing company that would dye huge quantities of yarn. If only a small number of skeins was needed, Gösta dyed the colors himself. Bohus Stickning yarns were initially dyed with plant dyes, but these soon gave way to synthetic dyes.

Emma loved the beautiful array of colors Bohus Stickning created. When a new color was developed, she would lovingly caress the skein and say, "Isn't it wonderful?" She paid the same loving attention to the completed garments on display in the Bohus Stickning headquarters. Marianne Erikson, textiles curator at The Röhss Museum of Arts and Crafts in Gothenburg, remembers Emma, then about ninety years old, coming to the museum, stroking a garment and saying, "I always liked this one."

An important aspect of Emma's duties as leader of the organization was to solicit customers. During its first years of operation, war restrictions limited Bohus Stickning's market base because tourism as well as textile exportation were sharply curtailed (Sweden was isolationist—no trade or tourism was allowed during World War II). Because of the high cost of production, Emma focused her efforts on acquiring and maintaining accounts with exclusive stores, many with a boutique-like atmosphere, that catered to upper-class Swedes. Emma worked closely with the shops to please the customers. If a particular sweater did not sell well, Bohus Stickning would exchange it for another design. If a customer needed a custom-made sweater or alteration, Bohus Stickning would accommodate.

Because the knitwear was expensive and considered a status symbol, Bohus Stickning was chided as being "not for the everyday citizen with a thin wallet". But, as noted by a critic in 1944, "First it has to be mentioned that the result is perfection. The material, the colors, patterns, and shapes are in all aspects complete, so outstanding and charming, that any type of criticism is meaningless."

After World War II, as economies recovered and tourists flocked to Sweden for vacations, Bohus Stickning launched its products into the international market, while maintaining its premier status in specialty shops and exclusive department stores. Sales soared.

Catering to the international market, information about Bohus Stickning was printed in French, German, and English: "Bohus Stickning is a Swedish Handicraft association centred [sic] in Gothenburg. This association promotes handknitted products only. The knitters mainly come from the stoneworkers' families of the Bohuslän province.

"Only the highest qualities of Swedish wool are used, selected by us and spun on small machines. The wool is dyed in a wide scale of colours [sic] to suit the manufacture of jumpers and cardigans as well as gloves and mittens, and caps for sporting and outdoor use. They are all made according to the many artistic designs belonging to the steadily increasing collection of Bohus knitting.

"This handicraft aims at the highest standard only."

Garments were exhibited in the United States, Tokyo, Düsseldorf, Paris, and Zürich. Customers came from far away places, including Switzerland, Canada, Mexico, and Bermuda. Recognizing that color preferences followed national boundaries (for example, Americans favored pastels and blues; Swedes, browns and blues; South Americans, pink), Bohus Stickning produced designs accordingly.

The shop in Gothenburg

could do more business in one day when

a cruise ship docked in port

than it did the rest of the month.

Tourism during the late 1940s and 1950s, especially by wealthy Americans, increased as large cruise liners docked in Gothenburg. Capitalizing on the opportunity, Emma helped produce a publicity film about Bohus Stickning to be shown on the cruise ships. In the film, a model tours the Bohus Stickning headquarters, visits with Emma, and watches Kerstin work on new knitting designs. The model then travels up the coast of the province and models various Bohus Stickning designs during a photo session. The film was a successful marketing tool and although business was always steady during the summer tourist season, the shop in Gothenburg could do more business in one day when a cruise ship docked in port than it did the rest of the month. More Bohus Stickning garments sold during the tourist season than the Christmas season.

Wanting to establish an export trade to the United States, in 1951 Emma made an agreement with Elizabeth Hanna of San Francisco to be sole distributor of Bohus Stickning garments in the country. Elizabeth took the garments to the most exclusive department stores and advised Emma on the needs of the United States market. Noting that many Americans collected Bohus Stickning sweaters, Elizabeth encouraged Emma to continue producing new designs. In 1956, Elizabeth imported more than 1200 garments and was Bohus Stickning's biggest account. Tragically, the United States' economy slumped and sales fell steadily over the following years. In 1959, Elizabeth sold only 314 garments, less than a third of the number sold three years earlier.

Bohus Stickning had a devastatingly difficult year in 1962 and only netted 404 kronor (approximately $77) in profit. Frustrated with the cyclic nature of Bohus Stickning problems, Emma explained to Elizabeth that a decrease in orders meant less work for their skilled knitters which resulted in their finding other employment, leaving Bohus Stickning with the expensive and time-consuming task of training new knitters. Emma concluded that only an increase in orders could prevent the loss of knitters and stabilize the industry. She urged Elizabeth to find more accounts in the United States, *"Everybody* says that there must be hidden possibilities in the USA. . ."

Seeing a considerable decline in orders from her customers in the early 1960s, Elizabeth was well aware of the problem. She wrote, "My only explanation of our current trouble with our old accounts is that the pattern of buying in America is very fickle. The old

Bohus Stickning knitwear on display at Nordiska Kompaniet (NK), a large department store in Stockholm.
Photograph courtesy of Ingrid Mesterton.

stores where quality has been important are changing to lure a very uncritical public quality-wise; but a public who is very conscious of all the latest style fads."

Several of the buyers Elizabeth worked with suggested that the garments be updated to fit changing fashion trends. One buyer was interested in a Chanel-style buttonless jacket sweater with 3/4-length sleeves that tapered with no ribbing, a straight hem with no ribbing, no ribbing on the front bands and a full-fashion sleeve. Another buyer had many ideas which Elizabeth passed on to Emma:

"The present buyer together with Mr. [Nieman] Marcus feel that the angora and EJA yarns are too limp in appearance to continue selling in America. Naturally, they feel they are several years ahead of the American trends, but definitely they will reject the present wools.

A model dons cardigan and pill box hat of "The Almond Tree" design by Kerstin Olsson. Photograph courtesy of Ingrid Mesterton.

"Her suggestions is that you try mohair and also the orlon and mohair mix available in Sweden. She feels that mohair takes dye even better than your yarns.

"Another suggestion is that the crocheted sweater is gaining over the knitted look. In this she recommends using mixed weights of yarns from the finest baby yarn to a normal fine.

"Another 'look' she recommends is the all-over afghan pattern or panels of the afghan pattern in soft natural wools.

"Lastly she mentioned that the rough texture but lacy look is the sophisticated answer to the rage for the bulky fisherman's sweaters and the re-appearance [sic] of tweeds in fashion.

"I'm sure all of this is no pleasure to read but imagine me having to listen and be polite!"

Emma liked the idea of the Chanel jacket because it could be varied infinitely in the future. But the recommendation to change fibers was not well received. Emma was justifiably proud of the quality and performance of their yarns and refused to make changes—the idea of replacing an angora-blend yarn with orlon and mohair seemed ludicrous. Probably in response to the suggestion of a rough textured but sophisticated version of the fisherman's sweater, Emma asked Karin Ivarsson to design some white-on-white patterns with a lot of depth.

Discouraged by the sales prospects for 1965, Elizabeth wrote to Emma:

"I have not felt in view of the U.S. market that I was justified in ordering this year . . . and I don't believe that I can again in the foreseeable future.

"If the rest of the world is going to follow American fad merchandising, I believe your volume will be affected negatively all throughout your sales area.

"I feel your production is very personal and must keep that way or be disbanded with dignity and not be cheapened."

Emma was naturally disappointed by Elizabeth's letter and wanted Elizabeth to develop a new marketing strategy. She wrote Elizabeth:

A model shows "The Cretan" designed by Emma. Photograph courtesy of Ingrid Mesterton.

"We do *not* either *need* a *distributor only, but a collaborator!* And a collaborator have you been all the years from 1951.

"You have meanwhile *not always been an easy collaborator* for us with regard to your often troublesome silence and your total secrecy in many questions about which information should have been desirable and very useful!

"Inspite [sic] of this did you give me the feeling that there was an activ [sic] personal friend on the other side of the hemisfere [sic] participating in our wants. All these statements were the cause that I—inspite [sic] of all difficulties you uttered—was *content when you assured me that you will abide with our decisions and most of all that you will not loose [sic] your interest* even though it does not appear very productiv [sic] at present.

"You speak of your interest, Elizabeth, which of course is of *moral* value—but I need most of all your *assistance* in these unforeseen difficulties and I feel sure, that your interest involves your aid. I do *need*

that you *are acting and seeking a way.*

"I consent with you that all selling must be done with *dignity.* I am farthermore [sic] of the opinion that one has to struggle in all difficulties. If these meanwhile are overwhelming inspite [sic] of all desire of 'eternity' one has to take the arduous task *with dignity to make an end!* We are as you see just now at the point of *struggling.*"

This, as all of Emma's letters to Elizabeth, conveys her persistent desire to succeed in the American market. The letter reveals not a sense of desperation, but rather an overwhelming conviction that Bohus Stickning could succeed. Emma and Elizabeth continued their correspondence about the United States market, but in 1966, they dissolved their business agreement.

The success of Bohus Stickning's designs was evident when their patterns began to be copied. In 1943, Vera Bjurström's design, "The Feather Stitch", was copied and used in a mitten by another company.

The offending company defended its actions, stating, "Because there is no protection of patterns in Sweden, this can happen to anybody. All companies produce items that are in demand. If we don't do it, someone else will." However, on the following day, the company agreed to stop production of the mitten out of a sense of allegiance to the Bohus knitters. Several other Bohus patterns were copied by other companies and although annoying to Emma and the designers, these copies were of obviously lower quality and did not seriously affect Bohus Stickning's sales.

In September of 1948, the popular American magazine, *Woman's Day*, featured ten original Bohus Stickning designs in an article entitled "Swedish Originals". The designs were not recognized as Bohus Stickning patterns, but were advertised as "Contemporary examples of traditional Scandinavian designs—these all knit with Swedish yarns. We've translated them into American materials so you may have them, too." The patterns were described in generic terms such as "gray on gray slipover" or "white with embroidered pattern mitten" and were estimated to cost the knitter about $5.40 and $1.20, respectively, in materials.

In 1961, the Danish Company, V. Juul Christensen and Son, produced a good-quality handknitted reproduction of "The Blue Shimmer" sweater which it sold at the international airport in Copenhagen. Elizabeth Hanna wrote to Emma that a prospective client ". . . had every intention of placing a small order but after a trip to New York wrote that she would not order as she understood the sweaters had been copied in Denmark."

Unaware of which Danish company was copying the design, Emma traveled to Copenhagen to investigate. After a couple of days, she received a tip to check out V. Juul Christensen and Son. On visiting their offices, Emma was a given a tour of their collection by "a very nice young man". Emma noted that their garments were of a very good quality (a high compliment from Emma). Finally, she saw the bogus Bohus garments and, feigning naiveté, she asked about them. She was told that they were Bohus but was quickly moved onto the next items. Emma so enjoyed her role as spy that she didn't reveal her identity.

Emma sent the results of her investigation to the firm's lawyer, Love Mannheimer. He contacted the Danish company and was successful in receiving an admission that their design "Jutland" was plagiarized from "The Blue Shimmer", and an agreement that they wouldn't imitate Bohus Stickning garments, including variations in color combinations, in the future. However, Christensen was granted permission to fill 3,500 orders for the plagiarized pattern before ceasing production. Emma suspected that the orders were not legitimate and was concerned about the impact 3,500 imitation garments would have on Bohus Stickning sales. Bohus Stickning, with total sales of 3,667 garments in 1961, was a much smaller firm than the Danish company which sold 30,000 garments.

The following year, three more Bohus Stickning patterns were copied and two Swedish magazines published plagiarized patterns. One picture caption read: "For you who dream about a sweater from Bohus Stickning, the white sweater with a yoke in colored patterns must be the perfect model." Emma's response: "We are constantly exposed to copies, and it is not fun to see patterns vulgarized in mass production."

Emma continued to be protective of the Bohus Stickning designs and wanted to stipulate that they could not be reproduced commercially until fifty years after her death.

"The Finnish Spike" designed by Emma shown in a cardigan and matching mittens.
Photograph courtesy of Ingrid Mesterton.

EMMA THE PERSON

It was Emma's strong will and determination that enabled her to help the women in the province find work and develop it into a successful business. One critic aptly reported that "Emma Jacobsson's special mark is the finicky way she chooses colors. She is acutely sensitive to colors and this is what has given Bohus Stickning its special artistic value. Emma Jacobsson has, as an expert of materials, artist, and production leader, mobilized all her personal resources . . . You could view the most exclusive garments as pure 'poems of color'."

Interestingly, Sigmund Freud had identified Emma's strong personality many years earlier. Unhappy with Emma's choice to study botany at the University, and wanting her to pursue a more traditional female field, Emma's father took her to see Freud, a personal friend. Rather than "correcting" Emma's career choice, Freud told Emma's father that she was of a very strong personality that was not easily influenced, and she should be allowed to follow the course of her choice.

This strong personality made Emma difficult to deal with at times. When upset about some difficulty with the company, Emma would slam the doors in her upstairs apartment, stomp down the stairs, and slam the door to her office. That action would clue the Bohus Stickning staff to keep busy at their jobs and avoid Emma until her mood changed.

Emma's attention to flawlessness was ingrained in her personality. Ingrid Mesterton, Emma's daughter, tells the story of her mother being hit by a car as she walked home from the library. (Evidently, Emma was so interested in the book she had borrowed that she didn't pay attention to the traffic.) Emma's leg was broken and she suffered a large cut on her head. On learning of her mother's accident, Ingrid picked five yellow roses from her mother's rose bushes to take to the hospital. Four of the roses matched perfectly, but the fifth was a different shade. After their visit, Emma asked her daughter to take the miscolored rose back home with her. Upon hearing this request, Ingrid knew that her mother was in no serious medical danger and that her mental capacity was fine—she was the perfectionist as always.

Ultimately, it was Emma's unrelenting pursuit of quality that enabled Bohus Stickning to achieve the high praise it received. She demanded and expected an enormous amount of dedication from her workers, designers, and knitters. But in return, she gave them respect, empathy, and a sense of pride. Because Emma was highly respected, she was able to make suggestions and changes in the designers' patterns without alienating them. She stimulated their creativity and encouraged them to experiment with colors, yarns, and patterns. Above all, Emma was an inspiration and friend to her colleagues.

Emma in the display room.
Photograph courtesy of Ingrid Mesterton.

One critic remarked,

"Emma Jacobsson's special mark is the finicky

way she chooses colors. . . .

You could view the most exclusive garments as

pure 'poems of color'."

Vera created embroidered designs influenced by Danish peasant embroidery. Vera was the only Bohus Stickning designer whose designs were never modified by Emma. From top, *"The Feather Stitch"* pullover courtesy of Bohusläns Museum, *"The Chain Seam"* mitten, *"The Slanting Square"* mitten, and untitled mitten courtesy of The City of Gothenburg Museum, and *"The Feather Stitch"* mitten and promenade sock courtesy of The Röhss Museum of Arts and Crafts. Photograph by Claes Jansson.

VERA BJURSTRÖM

Vera Bjurström and Emma Jacobsson were good friends before the beginning of Bohus Stickning. Vera had an artistic background and was a skilled seamstress, knitter, and embroiderer. When Emma was experimenting with different cottage industries, Vera helped by designing calico prototypes of stuffed animals. Later, when Bohus Stickning was established, Vera helped by designing knitting patterns. Vera volunteered her time and donated her designs to Bohus Stickning.

Initially, Vera experimented with two-color knitting designs, but she soon decided to concentrate on embroidered designs influenced by the Danish peasant embroidery that she had studied in school. The embroidered stitches were worked in a chain stitch to create a three-dimensional decoration on either a plain stockinette stitch or simple rib (K5, P2) background. They were worked with Rya wool, a 100% wool worsted-weight yarn. Vera was the only Bohus Stickning designer whose designs were never modified by Emma.

Vera's embroidered designs had two advantages. First, the embroidery embellished a knitted item while saving on yarn, which was very important during the war years. Second, the embroidered garments were produced in stages and provided income for more people. Knitters would construct the plain knitted garments, and after being approved at the Bohus Stickning headquarters, the garments were sent on to expert embroiderers to be embellished.

Vera was most active in Bohus Stickning during the first years of operation, when heavy sportswear, which lent itself well to embroidered embellishment,

This design by Vera uses the rib stitch throughout, but only the front is embroidered.
Photograph courtesy of Ingrid Mesterton.

was in demand. When finer weights of wool and angora yarns were introduced, the heavy sportswear lost popularity. Nonetheless, two of Vera's patterns, "The Feather-Stitch" and "The Slanting Square" became classic Bohus Stickning designs and were produced throughout its thirty-year operation.

*Anna-Lisa and a display of Bohus stickning garments from the early 1940s.
Emma admired Anna-Lisa's sensitivity to beauty and
remarkable sense of color and design.* Photograph courtesy of Ingrid Mesterton.

ANNA-LISA MANNHEIMER LUNN

Anna-Lisa Mannheimer Lunn, an enormously creative textiles enthusiast and avid knitter, was another of Emma's good friends. Emma admired Anna-Lisa's sensitivity to beauty and remarkable sense of color and design. On seeing some of her experimental knitting swatches—long strips of small colorful patterns—Emma asked Anna-Lisa to volunteer her designing expertise to Bohus Stickning. Anna-Lisa was eager not only to help her friend, but to experiment with the ever-increasing array of Bohus Stickning yarn colors. She volunteered her talents to Bohus Stickning through the early 1950s.

Anna-Lisa lived in Copenhagen and traveled to Gothenburg periodically to visit her relatives. On these trips, she would pick up an assortment of Bohus

Anna-Lisa's "The Blue Shimmer" was the most popular design and came to represent the characteristic style of Bohus knitwear. Photograph by Claes Jansson.

Stickning yarns which she would take back to Copenhagen with her to knit into long ribbons or swatches of patterns.

Anna-Lisa's designs were the first ones on which Emma collaborated. After Emma modified the pattern ribbon, the patterns were knit into the fronts of prototype cardigans that had plain, natural-colored sleeves and backs.

Designing with an array of colors was one of Anna-Lisa's passions. During the late 1940s, she began working with the angora-blend yarns and experimenting with new pattern placements. She introduced the yoke and inset yoke styles to Bohus Stickning. In 1947, she designed "The Blue Shimmer" which was the most popular design ever sold by Bohus Stickning and came to represent the characteristic style of Bohus knitwear.

Anna-Lisa's patterns were inspired by people and nature. Her design "Dean" was inspired by the famous black conductor, Dean Dixon who had worn a blue shirt that looked particularly beautiful with his dark skin tone. Anna-Lisa's pattern "The Red Edge" was inspired by sleeves she had knit for a leather jacket. Emma admired the sleeves and organized sections of the design into the popular sweater pattern.

A model wears Anna-Lisa's "The Stirrup". Photograph courtesy of Ingrid Mesterton.

"The Green Meadow" cardigan, "The Red Edge" pullover, mittens in "The Red Edge" and "The New Red Edge", and "The Flower Bed" gloves were designed by Anna-Lisa in the first half of the forties. *Photograph by Sixten Sandell.*

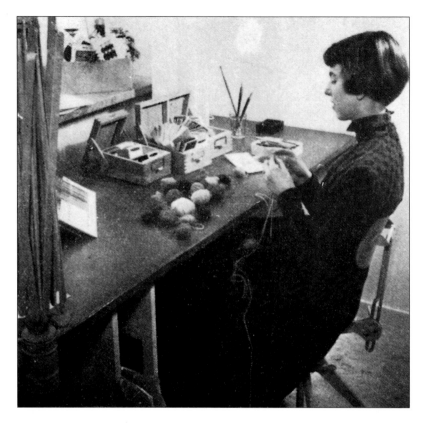

In 1952, Annika was the first designer hired by Bohus Stickning.
Photograph courtesy of Ingrid Mesterton.

ANNIKA MALMSTRÖM-BLADINI

In 1952, Annika, a student of design at Anders Beckman's School in Stockholm, was the first designer to be hired by Bohus Stickning on the recommendation of Göta Trägårdh (the color spy). She was hired to produce designs with the characteristic Bohus style established by Anna-Lisa's "The Blue Shimmer", but was not limited to this style.

Annika loved to work with colors, and was inspired by the ever-increasing array of hues of angora-blend yarns. She blended hues without harsh contrasts, using the same type of yarn throughout a design. Her patterns were so color specific that they could not be translated into different color combinations.

Some of Annika's designs, such as "The Spearhead", were complicated and required five colors in a single row. These designs were unpopular among the knitters, who were paid by the garment and not by the hour. Other designs, such as "The Zebra" were not of the characteristic Bohus style and prompted Kerstin Olsson to exclaim that Annika was ten years ahead of her time in designing such patterns.

Above: *Some of Annika's designs, such as "The Spearhead" pictured here, were complicated and required five colors in a single row.* Courtesy of The Röhss Museum of Arts and Crafts. Photograph by Claes Jansson.

Right: *"The Zebra", modeled here by Kerstin, who felt that Annika's designs were ten years ahead of the times.* Photograph courtesy of Ingrid Mesterton.

Annika worked in Gothenburg for Bohus Stickning for seven years, at which time she decided to work with printed fabrics instead. Although she enjoyed working for Bohus Stickning, she often felt isolated in her office day after day knitting swatches. Not wanting to lose a talented designer, Emma convinced Annika to work on a free-lance basis, designing one or two patterns a year for Bohus Stickning through the early 1960s.

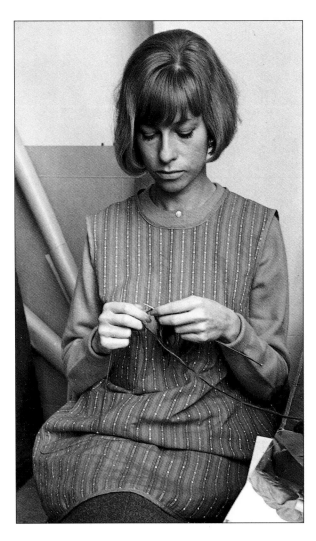

Kerstin Olsson designing at the Bohus Stickning headquarters. **Photograph courtesy of Ingrid Mesterton.**

KERSTIN OLSSON

Kerstin Olsson was introduced to Bohus Stickning when her design class from the Arts and Crafts School in Gothenburg visited the headquarters. Upon completion of her education in 1958, Kerstin's teacher arranged a meeting with Emma. Emma gave Kerstin a variety of yarns to knit into swatches, and liking the results, offered her a job. Like Annika, Kerstin was hired by Bohus Stickning in 1958 to create designs in the characteristic Bohus style.

Kerstin's first designs were done in only one color combination, that of her original design. For example, "The Wild Apple" was inspired by the clusters of berries on a mountain ash tree outside her studio at Bohus Stickning headquarters. The pattern had a dark green body with fifteen shades of oranges, reds, yellows, and greens in the yoke, and was knit with these colors only.

Kerstin's "The Egg" design was inspired by a paper-maché Easter egg that was presented to Emma from Edna Martin, a famous Swedish textiles artist and teacher, and her design class after being given a tour of the Bohus Stickning facility.

A trip to Paris in 1961 influenced Kerstin's later patterns, which then were translated into different colorways. On seeing gentle shadings of colors in ready-made clothing presented at fashion shows, Kerstin was inspired to experiment with shading in her knitting. These designs progressed from dark to light shades of a single color to produce a gradual intensification of that hue. These patterns were translated into various color combinations, such as "The Gray Mist", "The Green Mist", and "The Brown Mist".

Kerstin experimented with heavier yarns and simpler designs in the 1960s, producing the geometric black and white "Op" patterns. However, these

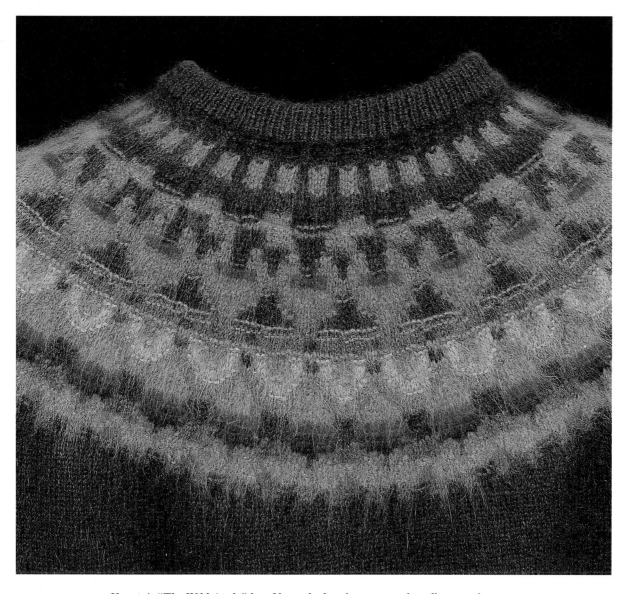

Kerstin's "The Wild Apple" has fifteen shades of oranges, reds, yellows, and greens.
Photograph by Claes Jansson.

patterns were not identified by the public as Bohus Stickning designs and were not popular.

Some of Kerstin's early designs contain three or four colors in a row. But Kerstin became sensitive to the fact that knitters were slowed down by so many color changes. Her later patterns, especially the shaded designs, contain only two colors per row. In an attempt to help the knitters, she incorporated plain rows in her designs to make increases and decreases more easily worked.

Emma considered Kerstin the least inhibited of the Bohus Stickning designers. Kerstin worked for Bohus Stickning until it closed in 1969.

Kerstin's inspiration for "The Mists" came from a 1961 fashion show of ready-made clothing in Paris. "The Brown Mist" sweater jacket and "The Green Mist" yoke pullover courtesy of The Röhss Museum of Arts and Crafts; "The Gray Mist" cowl neck pullover courtesy of Bohusläns Museum; "The Gray Mist" scarf privately owned.
Photograph by Claes Jansson.

Some of Kerstin's designs, including "Op" (right front).
Photograph by Claes Jansson.

Designer Karin Ivarsson wears "The Chain Seam",
designed by Vera. Photograph courtesy of Ingrid Mesterton.

KARIN IVARSSON

Karin Ivarsson contacted Bohus Stickning in 1959 after she finished design school at the Arts and Crafts School in Gothenburg. Although Karin had a small child, she needed a part-time position to help pay off student loans. Emma recognized Karin's potential and asked her to sketch some of her ideas for review. Being on a tight budget and unable to afford watercolor paper for the sketches, Karin painted several designs on pieces of crib liner. Emma liked Karin's ideas and sent her home with an assortment of yarn so that she could translate the designs into knitting.

Unfortunately, Karin was unable to make the conversion from painting to knitted design. Convinced of Karin's talent, Emma encouraged her to abandon the paints and to try swatching new designs with Bohus Stickning yarns. This method worked well and once or twice a month Karin brought her swatches to Bohus Stickning headquarters for Emma to evaluate and modify.

Karin's inspirations came from nature. "The Swan" was created after a bird-watching trip to the park with her young son. Her designs were translated into many different color combinations.

Taking advantage of Karin's design skills, Emma asked Karin to experiment with designs worked in all white. To add textural interest to the monochromatic designs, Karin incorporated different types of yarn. Though some of the resulting designs, such as "The Lagoon", were extremely difficult for the knitters to produce, the subtly textured sweaters were widely popular.

Karin continued to work for Bohus Stickning until its closure in 1969.

*Karin's design "The Swan", modeled by Kerstin, was inspired by a bird-watching trip
with her young son.* Photograph courtesy of Ingrid Mesterton.

Provincial knitters were organized in regional work centers. Photograph courtesy of Ingrid Mesterton.

THE KNITTERS

Of course, the success of Bohus Stickning was dependent on the knitters, and Emma strove diligently to meet their needs. During the first ten years of business, most of the knitters were the wives of fishermen and stone cutters looking for ways to supplement their families' depressed incomes. After World War II, as the economy improved and more jobs were available for women, the knitters tended to be women who loved the craft and longed to work with the beautiful yarns and patterns of Bohus Stickning.

Knitters were recruited throughout Bohuslän. Most were organized in regional work centers. A contact person was appointed from each of these work centers to act as liaison to Bohus Stickning headquarters.

Although most of them had been knitting since childhood, intensive courses were held at the work

Knitters were recruited throughout Bohuslän.
Photograph courtesy of Ingrid Mesterton.

centers to teach the workers how to knit for Bohus Stickning. They were taught about gauge, garment construction, yarn types, how to read the color graphs, and how to follow the schematic garment patterns and written instructions. Knitters were instructed on how to knit with two or three colors of yarn in the left hand and one color in the right—the left-hand yarns were "picked" and the right-hand yarn was "thrown".

Depending on the type of information presented, courses ran from two days to eight weeks with six hours of class time per day. Usually there were about fifteen students, but at times there were almost thirty. Courses were also taught for established knitters to learn new patterns and knitting techniques, and to make adjustments for different qualities of yarn. The classes were required and essential to help maintain the high-quality products associated with the Bohus Stickning label.

A worker presses a finished garment. Acceptable garments were washed and pressed before being displayed for sale. Notice the pressing cloth.
Photograph courtesy of Kerstin Olsson.

The group representative was a crucial figure in the Bohus Stickning chain of operation. Her job was time consuming and demanding, especially in the larger work centers. She was expected to know all of the knitting group members and their skill levels, and was responsible for making sure that garments were completed on time—knitters were not allowed to have a garment under construction for more than three months. (The majority of knitters completed one garment a month while the best knitters could do so in just fourteen days.) When there was a special order, the representative chose which knitters would fill it. Knitters who could fill the special order within fourteen days were given a 10-percent bonus.

When a new member joined a work center, she would knit a sample for the representative. If the knitter's skill was approved, the representative would supervise her in knitting three garments to submit to Bohus Stickning for Emma's approval.

The very skilled knitters worked on more than one garment at a time. For example, Ester Pettersson worked concurrently on three different designs, one of which was the intricate "The Wild Apple". Obviously, Ester was a superb knitter. While most knitters liked the variety of knitting different patterns, some preferred to specialize in just one or two patterns. Older knitters with declining vision often requested the designs that used light-colored yarn that was easier to see.

In most cases, a single knitter completed an entire garment. However, some knitters worked as teams, one working the patterned pieces while another worked the plain areas. Stina Josefsson was an excellent knitter who worked with her less experienced sister-in-law. While Stina knitted the patterned areas, her sister-in-law honed her skills on the plain sleeves and back.

After collecting a minimum of five completed garments, the representative would send them to the Bohus Stickning headquarters in Gothenburg along with a request for new projects for the knitters in her work center.

At the headquarters, each item was carefully evaluated to determine if it met Bohus Stickning standards. Critiques were written for each item and a copy returned with payment to the representative to forward to the knitter. Many of the critiques merely recognized good workmanship: "Fine Knitting" or "Very Fine Knitting". Others detailed mistakes:

"The cardigan 'The Forest Darkness' is nicely knitted but the garment is too small. You must have 169 stitches around the neck for a cardigan. You only have 157, no wonder it is too small. Will be paid as for size 44."

"The cardigan 'The Grayblue' is very nicely knitted, but the opening is not straight, deduct 3 kronor."

"The cardigan 'The Earnest' is nicely knitted. But the neckline is too small. The pattern is 10 cm wide, the yoke is 13 cm wide, so only 3 cm are left for the neck. [A little sketch was included with measurements.] Your knitting is nice otherwise. I'm sure this problem will not occur again."

The knitters became close circles of friends with knitting as their common goal.
Photograph courtesy of Ingrid Mesterton.

Garments that contained correctable mistakes were fixed by knitting experts at the Bohus Stickning headquarters, and the knitter's pay was reduced accordingly. During the 1950s and 1960s, garments with small defects were sold at a seconds store. The defect or error was clearly marked and the garment offered at a considerably reduced price. Garments with major errors such as a sweater with tension problems between the plain stockinette stitch body and the patterned yoke, were cut into pieces that were sent to retailers as pattern samples.

Knitters were paid by the piece, the amount depending on the design, type of garment, size, and quality. As with most labor-intensive occupations, handknitting commanded a low hourly wage. However, Bohus Stickning maximized the knitters' pay and gave increases often during its thirty-year operation. In 1941, when sweaters were first produced, a knitter earned 10 kronor ($2) for a cardigan, 1.9 kronor (36¢) for a pair of gloves, and 1.3 kronor (25¢) for a hat. By 1968, knitters earned five times as much or more for similar garments—56 kronor ($11) for a cardigan, 10 kronor ($2) for gloves, and 16 kronor ($3) for a hat—an increase greater than the rise in the cost of living. While the cost of coffee, apples, and milk doubled or tripled from 1941 to 1968, knitters' pay quintupled. The knitter's pay and benefits were always the highest component in the computation of the garment's cost.

The money earned by the knitters and representatives was essential supplemental income to household economies. This was the first money many women had ever received, and it gave them a sense of accomplishment and freedom to be able to buy a little something special for themselves. One knitter planned to purchase new coffee cups with her earnings. Another, Stina Josefsson, proudly used her earnings to purchase a heavy winter coat for 150 kronor ($29).

The representatives initially received 5 percent of the total amount of knitters' pay, plus mail and telephone reimbursements. Over the years, the representative's pay was gradually raised to 30 percent of her work center's production.

Each month, representatives gave the knitters in their work centers their pay, critiques, and yarn packets for new sweaters (containing the necessary colors and amounts of yarns, graph, and written instructions for a garment). Except at the work centers that covered very large areas (more than fifteen miles), the knitters gathered at monthly meetings to receive materials from their representatives, visit, and help each other with knitting problems. The knitters became close circles of friends with knitting as their common goal. In large areas, knitters met individually with the representative as their schedules permitted. One knitter biked 10 km (6 miles) with her daughter on the luggage rack in order to meet with her representative to exchange knitting projects.

Unlike those in the province, knitters who lived in Gothenburg scheduled appointments at the Bohus Stickning headquarters to receive their pay, critiques, and yarn for the next project. Gothenburg knitters received 10 percent higher salaries than those of the knitters in the province, probably because there were no representatives or mail expenses to pay.

In addition to their knitting earnings, Bohus knitters were given annual Christmas bonuses of 20 percent of their total yearly earnings. Some representatives held special parties in the middle of December to distribute these bonuses. Because bonuses were assured, knitters could borrow against them. In those

Bohus Stickning knitters were entitled to a week of relaxation at the vacation home at Härskogen.
Emma is eighth from the left standing.
Photograph courtesy of Ingrid Mesterton.

times of financial hardship, this flexibility was critical. One knitter borrowed 29 kronor ($6) against her bonus of 200 kronor ($39) to pay the maternity fee for the birth of her second child.

After earning its first net profits in 1947, Bohus Stickning established vacation pay as well as a week of vacation for all of its knitters. Knitters from each work center could spend one week at a vacation home with all expenses paid by Bohus Stickning. The vacation began with a stop in Gothenburg to tour the Bohus Stickning headquarters and visit with Emma Jacobsson and her staff. There, the knitters could see firsthand the Bohus Stickning headquarters, the business operation, and the variety of designs produced. Then they would go on to the vacation home at Härskogen for a week of relaxation. Although the vacation was offered to all the knitters, only those without family responsibilities were able to take advantage of the opportunity. (Anna-Lisa Mannheimer Lunn named a design after the vacation spot. It was a very popular design.)

Even though knitting had been chosen for a cottage industry because it could be produced on a continuous basis, production tended to be seasonal. Socks and mittens were produced year round, but sweater production peaked during November, February, and March. Knitters were busy with family obligations during the Christmas season, and during the summer they had to help with farming activities. In addition, many of the rural knitters moved to their basements during the summer months, renting their homes to wealthy city people for extra income. The minimal lighting in the basements made knitting difficult. To encourage knitters to meet the product demand during these months, Bohus Stickning paid its knitters bonuses for fast delivery.

The number of knitters working for Bohus Stickning peaked at 870 in 1947. Although Bohus Stickning conducted classes to teach techniques and standards, most of the knitters had learned to knit as young girls and had been knitting all their lives. For many of the women, knitting was a labor of love. That it allowed them to earn some extra income was sheer delight.

Ester Pettersson, who began knitting for Bohus stickning in 1956, said in a 1962 radio interview that although the patterns were difficult, they were also interesting and fun. She was a fast knitter and completed a garment every fourteen days (more than 150 sweaters in the six years she knit for Bohus Stickning). Ester estimated that she knitted an average of eight to ten hours a day depending on what household chores she had to complete. She loved the craft and found the long hours of knitting to be relaxing. Moreover, she was stimulated by the various patterns, colors, and yarns. She often worked on more than one garment at a time and believed "The Wild Apple" to be the most beautiful Bohus Stickning design.

Another knitter shared Ester's enthusiasm for Bohus Stickning: "It is so exciting to see pattern after pattern grow and then form a unity. When they are done, they are complete works of art . . ."

Of course, not all of the knitters found the work enjoyable. One knitter described it as the work of the devil and did it only for the income it provided. Another prolific but weary knitter complained that if she had kept all the things she had knit for Bohus Stickning, she wouldn't have been able to walk into her house.

Sales of Bohus Stickning garments peaked in 1957, but in the dozen years that followed, the organization was plagued with problems and sales dropped. Each time a problem arose, Emma took out a piece of paper and listed the nature of the problem in one column and possible solutions in another column. This is how Emma came up with the idea to pay a higher fee to the knitters when the organization needed to increase production of special orders, and to look into new international markets when they needed to expand their customer base. Late in the 1960s, the problems were many and complex. Emma neatly listed seven problems in an organized column but had no solutions to place next to them.

First was the general depression in the market caused by a reduction in tourism and the devaluation of Swedish currency. Not only had tourism declined, but the type of tourist had changed. Wealthy American tourists with vast expendable incomes had been replaced by middle-class Americans traveling on tight budgets.

Second was a decrease in the number of knitters. Although Bohus Stickning had increased knitter's salaries, they were still paid very little in relation to the number of hours they worked on a garment. In an attempt to keep up with demand and reduce production costs, Bohus Stickning tried to have the plain parts of the garments knitted by machine. But the hand- and machine-knit portions did not combine well enough to carry the Bohus Stickning label.

Many abandoned knitting for the various new jobs that were opening up in urban areas. Others were discouraged by new tax laws that lowered the amount of profit that they could make from work done at home. Emma even believed that the introduction of television contributed to the declining number of knitters.

Third, orders from old customers decreased and were not offset by new customers. Retailers were becoming increasingly reluctant to carry expensive garments that did not sell quickly. Wholesale prices for Bohus Stickning garments were high to begin with and by the time retailers tripled these prices, which was customary, the garments were too pricey for most shoppers.

In attempts to reduce wholesale costs, Emma experimented with coarser yarns and simpler patterns, but these designs were not as popular as the very complicated and beautiful angora-blend garments associated with the Bohus Stickning label. Wages were eventually reduced for the staff and designers at the Bohus Stickning headquarters, but costs remained high, largely because the knitted items that did not meet Emma's high standards were rejected and Bohus Stickning had to absorb the cost.

Fourth was a change in fashion tastes. Single-colored machine-knit mohair sweaters became the fashion rage, inexpensive man-made fibers gained wide popularity, and consumers came to value cheap prices over durability and quality. The disposable society was coming of age.

Fifth was a decrease in the availability of high quality wool. Ranchers had begun to cross-breed sheep to increase their meat production. This resulted in a decrease in wool quality. Fortunately, Bohus Stickning had a large stockpile of angora yarns for their most popular garments, but it would be exhausted in just a couple of years. After that, they would be forced to work with inferior wool.

The sixth and seventh reasons were related to the

organizational structure of Bohus Stickning. In hindsight, Emma wished that Bohus Stickning had formed an alliance with another group, such as the association that made bobbin lace, as an avenue to cooperatively market their products. Emma felt that the organization's survival hinged on finding knowledgeable advisors to help produce and market the garments.

At age eighty-four, Emma was also contemplating retirement, though she did not list this as one of the seven pressing problems. Back in 1957, Emma had looked for someone to take over the industry and hopefully rejuvenate it. However, because the salary was modest and Emma's standards were high, a suitable replacement was not found. In 1969, the situation repeated itself.

After much agonizing, the difficult decision to close Bohus Stickning was made. On January 30, 1969, Emma Jacobsson wrote the following letter to the knitters:

Dear Knitters,

Maybe you have heard the rumors about the difficulties of Bohus Stickning which means that the company can no longer continue. After many considerations we have decided, with sorrow, that Bohus Stickning has to cease its production. The same difficulties that other textiles companies in Sweden have met led to this result. With this letter we would like to inform you about the situation.

The reasons for our decision are many. It has to do with the new times and the high prices created by our technique, handknitting, and the high quality of the material. Another reason is the catastrophically decreasing amount of high quality fine wool which makes it impossible in the future to produce our angora yarns, which are the yarns used almost exclusively for our products today.

We have experimented with changes in our production by using other materials and different styles and techniques, but the production has not been as popular as we hoped for. This is probably due to the special Bohus Stickning character being lost with new materials and techniques.

We will not close the business immediately but will continue until the end of April. Therefore, we request that your last work be completed and sent to us before the end of March. We hope by the end of March you will have time to knit as many garments as possible in the best quality as possible. After the orders from Bohus Stickning have been fulfilled by you, we hope that you continue to knit for yourselves with the yarns that you have bought from us. Naturally you understand that it is of utmost importance to all of us, for you and our personnel in Gothenburg, that during the remaining months we continue our usual intensive and good cooperation and that during this time everybody, in their own way, seek to contribute so Bohus Stickning can fulfill its work in an honorable way and not lose its good reputation.

We have sought contacts with other large companies with better resources than ours for a takeover to continue our production. Regrettably we have not been successful, probably due to the fact that handknitted products are for the moment hard to sell. We find comfort in knowing that the situation from the time we started Bohus Stickning has totally changed in Sweden, which has contributed to work opportunities for women to a much greater extent. We believe that Bohus Stickning during its thirty-year span has been a help and support for the women of the province.

It is with deep sorrow that we are forced to lay down this inspiring production and this fine and stimulating cooperation with all of you. We thank you for your cooperation during the thirty years which cannot be expressed enough.

For Bohus Stickning,

Emma Jacobsson

At their last group meeting, each knitter was given a packet of Bohus Stickning yarn as a closing gift. Throughout its thirty years of operation, Bohus Stickning brought much fulfillment and pleasure to its knitters by way of earnings, vacations, beautiful yarns and patterns to knit, and through social interaction. The feelings of gratitude and respect on the part of the knitters are made clear by excerpts from knitters' letters to Bohus Stickning with regards to its closure:

Thank you from my heart for the going away gift, the beautiful yarn. It was a big surprise for me. When I see the yarn I remember my first cardigan for you, it was "The Blue Stripe" and the year was 1949.

This should thus be the last sweater. It is sad but nothing we can do anything about. That's life. Left is only to thank you for all the twenty-three years.

I would like to thank you so much for all these twenty-two years that I have had the opportunity to be a knitter for Bohus Stickning. It has given me much joy and benefits. I have often thought with gratefulness and admiration of Mrs. Jacobsson who started this organization.

I am sending the last garment to Bohus Stickning. I have knitted 661 garments since I started on November 11, 1948.

This is something you wouldn't even dream about, to get Bohus yarn for the whole family.

It will be a big loss not to get Bohus knitting anymore. It had been so interesting and nice when sitting alone. . .

Bohus Stickning officially ceased operations on April 30, 1969.

EPILOGUE

The decision to close Bohus Stickning was devastating to Emma who had devoted thirty years to the business. Furthermore, the closure rekindled Emma's memories of the failure of her family's glove business due to economic weaknesses after World War I. She had hoped never to relive those depressing times.

Upon closure of the business, Emma donated Bohus Stickning garments, pattern cards, sketchbooks, yarn samples, and pattern swatches to The Röhss Museum of Arts and Crafts and The City of Gothenburg Museum.

Emma remained consumed with Bohus Stickning even after its closure and began work on a book about its history. To fill in details that she might have forgotten, Emma asked key people who had worked with Bohus Stickning to write about their involvement. A compilation of much of this information is presented in a thesis written in 1977 by Ulla Häglund, a student at the Institute of Arts and Sciences at Gothenburg University.

Emma Jacobsson died in 1977 when she was ninety-three years old. As a tribute to her, mourners at her funeral wore black Bohus sweaters.

True to her scientific nature, Emma had documented all aspects of the Bohus Stickning business. After Emma's death, her daughter, Ingrid Mesterton, arranged to have the business records and files organized and catalogued, and then donated them to The Women's Archives at the Gothenburg University Library. Ingrid and Kerstin Olsson also contributed to the collection of Bohus Stickning knitwear given to the Bohusläns Museum in Uddevalla.

In 1980, several exhibits of Bohus Stickning knitwear were shown in Sweden. Money from the closure of Bohus Stickning was used to fund a book, *Bohus Stickning*, about the history of the organization. Ulla Häglund, who had written her thesis about Bohus Stickning and later became textiles curator of The City of Gothenburg Museum, authored the book with additions by Ingrid. The book, designed to provide supplemental information for the Bohus Stickning exhibits, is no longer in print.

Proceeds from *Bohus Stickning* were used to establish the Emma Jacobsson Stipend which is awarded annually to an artist who received his/her training at the Arts and Crafts School in Gothenburg. The first award was given in 1988. Kerstin Olsson was appropriately awarded the stipend in 1989.

Kerstin Olsson continued her artistic career after the closure of Bohus Stickning. She is currently an appliqué and watercolor artist in Gothenburg.

Karin Ivarsson has continued in the textiles field as a weaving instructor at a community center in Angered, a suburb of Gothenburg.

In the fall of 1994, five women who were members of the work center in Uddevalla met at the Bohuslän Museum to reminisce about their involvement with Bohus Stickning. They were Stina Josefsson, age seventy-five; Ingrid Andersson, sixty-six; Ingegärd Edwardsson, seventy-six; Daga Torstensson, sixty-nine; and Ingegärd Larsson, seventy-eight. All five of these women came to knit for Bohus Stickning by answering newspaper ads placed by their work center representative. With the exception of Ingrid, all worked for Bohus Stickning for five to seven years from the late 1940s to mid 1950s. Ingrid knit for three years in the early 1960s.

When these women worked for Bohus Stickning, they were young mothers in their late twenties and early thirties. They recalled getting up early or staying up late to knit the intricate patterns while their children slept. Some put their children to bed early so that they could meet deadlines. Because all of these women had family obligations, none were able to attend a vacation provided by Bohus Stickning. None of these women was ever able to visit the Bohus Stickning headquarters in Gothenburg or meet Emma Jacobsson. For them, travel expenses were just too high.

Years later, these knitters maintained fond appreciation for the beauty of Bohus Stickning designs and yarns. Though most of the knitters were forced to end their association with Bohus Stickning when the birth of an additional child left them with no extra time for knitting, they all agreed that if the opportunity existed today, they would knit again for Bohus Stickning.

THE BOHUS
STICKNING GARMENTS

Bohus Stickning produced a wide variety of knitwear: mittens, socks, gloves, scarves, hats, berets, and sweaters. The first garments were knitted of natural-colored wool, but soon colorful patterns became the hallmark of Bohus Stickning.

MITTENS WITH KNIT-IN MOTIFS

Mittens were made of finger-weight wool yarn and generally had reverse stockinette stitch cuffs that were brushed to raise a luxurious loft. Color patterns were usually confined to the back of the mitten hand. Cuffs, palms, and fingertips were generally knit in the color that was used as background for the color pattern on the back of the hand.

EMBROIDERED MITTENS

Most of the embroidered mittens were knit from worsted- or sport-weight wool yarn, and had a K1, P1 rib cuff. The cuff and fingertip were commonly worked in a contrasting color. All of the embroidered designs were created by Vera with the exception of one which

Emma designed. The embroidered designs were restricted to the back of the hand—many of the motifs were three-dimensional and would not have been practical elsewhere. In many designs, the back of the mitten hand was worked in a K6, P2 or K5, P2 rib as a base for the embroidery.

GLOVES

Gloves were constructed from finger-weight wool yarns, and had either brushed, reversed stockinette stitch, or K1,P1 cuffs. They were patterned on the backs and had solid-color fingers and palms.

GAUNTLET GLOVES

Gauntlet gloves were generally knit from angora-blend yarns. They had turned-back stockinette stitch hems that were folded over a single purl row. The hands were knit in a single color and the gauntlets were patterned. Gauntlet length ranged from 1" to 5", and some of the longer ones flared from 3" wide at the wrist to as much as 6" at the end of the cuff.

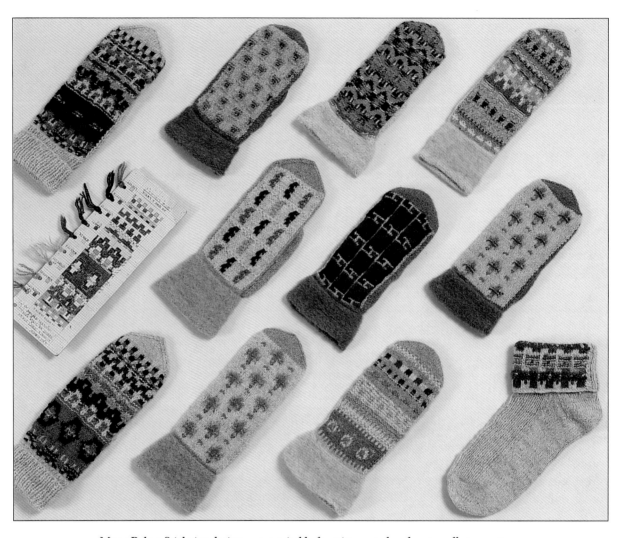

Many Bohus Stickning designs were suitable for mittens and socks, as well as sweaters.
From right to left, starting at top row:
"Härskogen" by Anna-Lisa, "The Blue Tone" by Annika, "The Window" by Emma, courtesy of The City of Gothenburg Museum;
"The New Red Edge" by Anna-Lisa, privately owned; "The Cross" by Anna-Lisa, courtesy of The Röhss Museum of Arts and Crafts; "The Stairs"
and "The Finnish Spike" by Emma, courtesy of The City of Gothenburg Museum; "The Blue Edge" pattern card and "The Green Meadow" sock
by Anna-Lisa, privately owned; "Capri" by Anna-Lisa, courtesy of The City of Gothenburg Museum; "The Cross" by Anna-Lisa, courtesy of The
Röhss Museum or Arts and Crafts; and "The Gold Edge" by Anna-Lisa, privately owned. Photograph by Claes Jansson.

SOCKS

Socks were constructed from sport- and worsted-weight wool yarns. The toe, bottom of the foot, and heel were worked in stockinette stitch, and the top of the foot and leg in K1, P1 rib. The promenade or fancy socks were similar with the exception of patterned turn-down cuffs. These patterns were either knit in stockinette stitch or embroidered onto a K5, P2 rib with the same patterns used for the mittens.

SCARVES

Scarves were knit from angora-blend yarns in seed stitch. Fancy scarves had patterned ends, some of which were folded over and hemmed, making the scarves reversible. Other designs were bordered at the ends with seed stitch to prevent the pattern from rolling under. Because the seed stitch border was limited to the ends, the patterns tended to roll in a bit along the sides.

HEADWEAR

Berets, caps, pill box hats, pixie hats, and head scarves were mostly knit from angora-blend yarns. Berets and caps were worked circularly from the ribbing to the crown, and were patterned along the sides and, in some designs, on the crown.

The sides of the pill box hats were patterned and the crowns were worked in solid colors. On some of these hats, a small tuck was sewn between the crown and the straight sides to give the shape more definition.

The lower halves of pixie hats were worked in the round just as the other hats, and then a number of

Berets were worked circularly from
the ribbing to the crown.

From the top, clockwise: *"The Turquoise"*, *"The Trumilen Green"*, *"The Willow Brown"* and *"The Gold Mist"* by Kerstin, courtesy of The Röhss Museum of Arts and Crafts; *"The Coral"* by Kerstin, courtesy of Bohusläns Museum; *"The Flame"*, *"The Garnet"*, and *"The New Azalea"* by Kerstin, *"The Forest Darkness"* by Annika, and *"The Grillwork"* by Kerstin, courtesy of The Röhss Museum of Arts and Crafts. Photograph by Claes Jansson.

*"The Flower Bed",
designed by Anna-Lisa,
shown in scarf, mittens,
and promenade socks.*
Photograph courtesy of
Ingrid Mesterton.

stitches were bound off at the center. The remaining stitches were worked back and forth for the desired length and then bound off. This bound-off edge was folded in half and sewn together, and a wire was inserted into the seam to give a little pixie curve to the top of the hat. The seam was centered over the first bound-off stitches, and the side edges were sewn to the first bound-off stitches. The pattern was worked either on the entire hat or was limited to the lower part that was worked in the round.

Bohus Stickning produced two varieties of head scarves. The most popular had a triangular shape. Triangular head scarves were worked back and forth in stockinette stitch with a knit-in pattern above a K1, P1 rib at the lower edge. The sides were decreased evenly to form the point.

The other type of head scarf looked like a headband with a triangular extension at the back. It fit the head snugly. It was worked much the same as the pixie hat, with the headband part worked circularly for the desired length, and then the scarf part worked back and forth as the side edges were decreased to form a triangle. This "tail" gradually curved to a rounded end which was worn tucked under the headband in the back.

The pixie hat, shown at left, had a wire inserted into the seam to give a little curve to the top of the hat.
"The Red Palm" pullover by Kerstin, courtesy of Bohusläns Museum; "The Watermelon" yoke cardigan and cap and "The Star" yoke pullover by Kerstin, and "New Bohus Granite" pixie hat and gauntlet gloves by Anna-Lisa, courtesy of The City of Gothenburg Museum.
Photograph by Claes Jansson.

The most popular head scarf was triangular.
The sides were decreased evenly to form the point.
Photograph courtesy of Ingrid Mesterton.

"The Chain Seam"
by Vera.
Photograph courtesy of
Ingrid Mesterton.

SWEATERS

Over the years, a variety of changes were made to the pullovers and cardigans. The garments were constructed from finewool or EJA yarn and, late in the 1940s, angora yarns. During the first decade of production, sweaters were worked flat and had patterned fronts with natural-color stockinette stitch backs, sleeves, and ribbing. The sweaters were short, about waist length, with considerable shaping at the side seams. The fronts of the sweaters were wider than the backs so that the side seams fell slightly in back of the underarm seam of the set-in sleeves. Embroidered sweaters were shaped and worked similarly with the exceptions that the back, sleeves, and ribbing were sometimes navy and the embroidery usually extended only to the underarm shaping. The fronts were worked in plain stockinette stitch, K6, P2 rib, or intarsia blocks of color. The embroidery was done with two strands of Rya yarn.

Over the years, Bohus Stickning made many changes to their designs. Some were the result of fashion trends, such as changes in sweater shaping. Others resulted from advances in technology, such as the use of angora-blend yarns and synthetic dyes. Still others came about as Emma and the designers experimented with ways to perfect and enhance their product. These experiments included pattern placement and color combinations.

Beginning in 1949, Anna-Lisa began to experiment with different styles of sweater bodies and pattern placements. She introduced the yoke sweaters, referred to as "old round knitting", and the inset-yoke sweaters, called "new round knitting".

Yoke pullovers and cardigans were worked circularly from the neck down to the armhole. To make the sweaters fit better, short rows were worked back and forth at the base of the yoke. Then the stitches were divided between the front, back, and sleeves and the components were completed by knitting back and forth. Cardigan yokes were worked back and forth with simultaneous working of the buttonband ribbing. Short rows and sweater body were worked the same as the pullover.

During the late 1940s and early 1950s, the yoke sweaters had considerable shaping at the side seams—about two inches on each side. By the 1960s, fashion demanded less fitted sweaters, so the shaping along the side seams was eliminated.

Inset-yoke sweaters were worked back and forth from the bottom up, leaving a scooped neck opening.

After the shoulder seam was sewn, stitches for the yoke were picked up along the neck opening and worked circularly. Then the sleeves were set in. The yoke of an inset-yoke sweater was much shallower than that of a yoke sweater. Like the yoke sweaters, the inset-yoke sweaters initially had a lot of shaping along the side seams which was omitted during the late 1950s.

Many designs were adapted so that they could be used for both styles of sweaters. For example, the yoke sweater designs "Dean" and "Bumblebee" were modified for inset-yoke sweaters and named "Little Dean" and "Little Bumblebee".

The yoke sweaters were the most popular garments produced by Bohus Stickning and the majority of patterns were made for this shaping. But in response to fashion changes in the early 1960s, Bohus Stickning developed some new styles. One was a jacket in which the side fronts were knit sideways and the backs and sleeves were knit from the bottom up. The edges were worked in garter stitch and the sleeves

The two inset-yoke sweaters, shown at far left, were worked back and forth from the bottom up, leaving a scooped neck opening. After the shoulder seams were sewn, stitches for the yoke were picked up along the neck opening and worked circularly.

Photograph courtesy of Ingrid Mesterton.

The yoke sweater designs for "The Bumblebee" and "Dean" were created by Anna-Lisa. They were also modified for inset yoke sweaters.

"The Bumblebee" courtesy of Bohusläns Museum, "Dean" courtesy of The Röhss Museum of Arts and Crafts. Photograph by Claes Jansson.

"The Swan", by Karin, is shown at left in a jacket. The side fronts were knit sideways and the backs and sleeves were knit from the bottom up.

Cardigan jacket courtesy of Bohusläns Museum, "The Swan" sweater, "The Large Collar" tam, and gauntlet gloves courtesy of The Röhss Museum of Arts and Crafts. Photograph by Claes Jansson.

were set in. Another design was for a plain-bodied hemmed sweater with a large patterned cowl neck, and some had patterned bands at the wrists. Bohus Stickning also experimented with drop shoulder sweater shapes. In some sweaters, the patterns were limited to the lower edge, and in others were worked all over, as in "Op". These garments had hemmed sleeves, necklines, and lower edges, and were not shaped along the side seams.

Knitting instructions and garment designs were passed on to the knitter through the knitting courses sponsored by Bohus Stickning. The written instructions are vague by today's standards—the necessary details must have been covered in the classes. The instructions gave the basic directions for all garments of a particular style, such as tams, cardigans, yoked pullovers, etc., and were not specific to any particu-

lar design. Because finewool, Finn wool, EJA, angora, and Q-yarns had similar gauges of about 9 stitches per inch, they could be interchanged. Only Rya yarn, with a gauge of approximately 5 stitches per inch, required separate instructions.

In addition to written instructions, knitters were given a pattern card that illustrated the color design as well as the number of rows, stitches, increases, and decreases to be worked in the pattern repeat. Separate cards were made for each type of garment constructed out of each pattern. For example, three cards were made of the pattern "The Large Collar", one each for gauntlet gloves, a hat, and a yoke sweater.

These designs have large patterned cowl necks and a patterned band at the lower edge.
Some designs had patterned bands at the wrists as well.
"The Lagoon" cowl neck pullover (at rear) and pill box hat, and "The Twisted Pattern" cowl neck pullover (at right) by Karin,
courtesy of The Röhss Museum of Arts and Crafts; "The Pale Shimmer" cowl neck pullover and scarf by Anna-Lisa,
courtesy of Bohusläns Museum. Photograph by Claes Jansson.

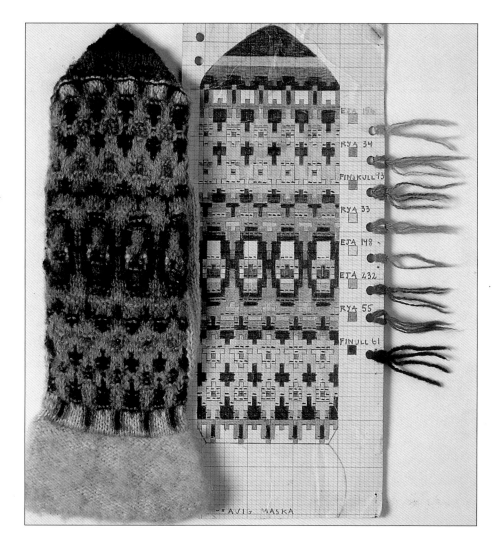

Knitters were given a pattern card that illustrated the color design as well as the number of rows, stitches, increases, and decreases to be worked in the pattern repeat. Shown here is "Scilla" by Anna-Lisa.

Photograph courtesy of The Women's Archives at Gothenburg University.

Pattern cards contained graphs of different sections of a pattern, with varying instructions for increases and decreases, depending on the garment. For example, the graph for a yoke sweater of "The Large Collar" included the entire pattern length and was annotated with instructions for where increase rows should be worked. The graph for a jacket of "The Large Collar" also included the entire pattern length, but because no shaping was done in the patterning, instructions for increase rows were not necessary. The graph of the same design for gauntlet gloves was only an abbreviated length of the pattern and was annotated as to where decreases should be worked for shaping the gauntlet. All of these graphs were read in the same way, although some contained more information than others.

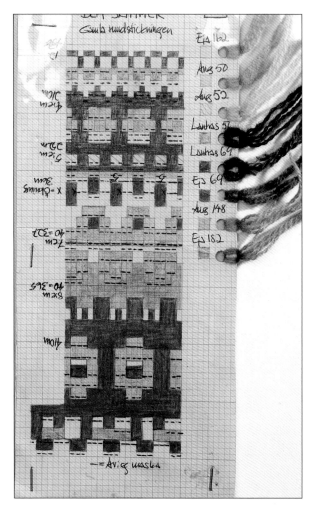

Pattern card for "The Blue Shimmer".
Each square on the graph represents one stitch and each
line represents one row or round of knitting. The card was
read from right to left and bottom to top. For the yoke
sweaters, which were worked from the neck down, the pat-
tern card was rotated 180°.
Courtesy of Ingrid Mesterton.

Each square on a graph represented one stitch and each line represented one row or round of knitting. At the center top of the pattern card was the name of the design. Under the name on some of the cards was a description of the garment to be made from that card (such as "old round knitting" for a yoke sweater). A graph key, color codes, and yarn samples were given in the right-hand margin. Increases and/or decreases were marked in the left-hand margin. A key for purl stitches was given at the bottom center of the card. All of the graphs were read from right to left and bottom to top. Because the yoke sweaters were worked from the neck down, the graphs were read from the last row in the design to the first row. By rotating the pattern card 180°, the last row in the design was at the bottom of the card and the graph could be read from right to left and bottom to top, as usual. Pattern cards for yoke sweaters were identified with the words "old round knitting", and increase designations written upside down along the left margin. When the card was rotated so that the pattern could be read bottom to top, the increase markings were in the right margin and right-side up.

A dash (–) in a square indicated that the stitch should be purled on a knit row or knit on a purl row. An open square indicated a stitch that should be knit on a knit row and purled on a purl row.

The increase or decrease numbers along the side of the graphs instructed the knitters how many stitches were needed in that particular row. Some of these numbers indicated the exact number of stitches that should be increased. Others indicated the intervals at which increases should be worked (every fifth stitch, for example). The knitter had to be aware of the final number of stitches required in an increase or decrease row because she could seldom increase or decrease evenly across the row and come up with the correct number of stitches. Increases and decreases were to be worked evenly across a row, and at least ten stitches away from the buttonband on a cardigan.

In addition, the knitter had to keep in mind the number of stitches in a pattern repeat, particularly in yoke sweaters which were not to have partial motifs. The knitter would use the increase notations along the side of the graph to estimate the number of stitches needed, but would make adjustments along the entire yoke for the pattern. For example, using the pattern card for a yoke sweater of "The Blue Shimmer", the knitter had to make the adjustments shown in the chart below to obtain the correct number of stitches.

Although these changes may seem small and unimportant for much of the yoke, they were necessary if there was to be an entire repeat of the final motif in the graph. If these adjustments were not made and there was a partial repeat of a motif, the knitter's pay would be reduced.

ADJUSTMENTS KNITTER HAD TO MAKE TO "THE BLUE SHIMMER" INSTRUCTIONS TO ACHIEVE CORRECT NUMBER OF STITCHES.

instructions	no adjustments 156 sts	adjustments 156 sts
After working the ribbing, increase	12 sts	12 sts
On row #11, inc every 4th st	42 sts	42 sts
Sub-total	210 sts	210 sts
On row #18, inc every 5th st	42 sts	42 sts
Sub-total	252 sts	252 sts
On row #26, inc every 7th st	36 sts	36 sts
Sub-total	288 sts	288 sts
On row #34, inc every 7th st	41 sts	42 sts (+1 st)
Sub-total	329 sts	330 sts
On row #37, adjustment in sts for pattern repeat	0 sts	6 sts (+6 sts)
Sub-total	329 sts	336 sts
On row #43, inc every 8th st	41 sts	42 sts (+1 st)
Sub-total	370 sts	378 sts
On row #51, inc for a total of 410 sts	40 sts	32 sts (-8 sts)
Sub-total	410 sts	410 sts
On row #63, adjustment in sts for pattern repeat	0 sts	22 sts (+22 sts)
Grand Total	410 sts	432 sts

Below is an example of the brief knitting instructions given to the knitters in 1949 for a Woman's pullover constructed from Rya yarn.

Work Instructions for Ladies Pullover
sizes 40 (42) 44 (46)
for Rya yarn

Front Piece: CO 140 (140) 150 (160) sts on size 000 needles and work 1 × 1 ribbing for 10 cm. Change to #0 needles and stockinette stitch, increase in first row evenly 10 sts (for size 40 do not make incs after the ribbing). The smoothest inc should be used (for very tight knitting use #1 needles). Increase thereafter 1 st each side every 8th row, until the work measures 46 (50) 54 (58) cm wide. When the work measures 31 (32) 33 (34) cm long, BO for armhole, about 12, 6, 4, 2, 1 sts in each side, the work should measure 36 (37) 38 (39) cm wide. When the work measures 44 (45) 46 (47) cm long (13 cm from armhole bind off), place the center 20 sts on a thread. Work each side, BO about 6, 4, 3, 2, 1 sts. Knit even until armhole measures 19 cm. BO for shoulder in three batches about 39–42 sts depending on the size.

Back Piece: CO 120 (120) 130 (140) sts on size 000 needles and knit 10 cm of 1 × 1 ribbing. Change to #0 needles and st st, increase in the first row evenly 10 sts (not for size 40). Increase in the side like for the front piece until it measures 40 (44) 48 (52) cm wide. At 31 (32) 33 (34) cm BO for armhole until you have the same number of sts as the front piece.

When the armhole measures 18 cm, BO for shoulder in three groups.

Long Sleeve: CO 18–20 sts on #0 needles and knit in st st. Inc 1 st in the beg and end of each row until there are 44 sts. Inc 1 st beg of every row until the crown measures 16 cm. CO 3 sts at the end of two rows or 5–7 sts in 2 rows depending on the size. The sleeve width for the different sizes should be 36 (37) 38 (39) cm. Dec 1 st each side every 8th row, when the work measures 55 cm, change to #000 needles and 1 × 1 ribbing for 8 cm. Dec in the first row to 76 sts. BO loosely, purl over purl, knit over knit.

3/4 Length Sleeve: Make like the long sleeve. The sleeve width should be 1 cm smaller. Dec 1 st each side every 6th row. When the work measures 40 cm, change to #000 needles and ribbing, dec to 86 sts, work 1 × 1 ribbing for 4 cm. BO.

Short Sleeve: Work the same as the 3/4 length sleeve but 1 cm smaller in sleeve width. Dec 1 st in each side every 4th row. When the work measures 23 cm change to #000 needles and ribbing, dec to 98 sts, knit 1 × 1 rib for 2 cm. BO.

Finishing: Sew all the seams together with close backstitch. Sew the sleeves to the middle of the sleeve crown at the shoulder seam, place the sleeve seam slightly in front of side seam. Sew in all threads.

Neckband: Pick up about 140–146 sts around the neck (just 1 st for each purl st and 1 st for each row on the side). Knit one plain row, then 1 × 1 ribbing for 5 cm. BO loosely in knit and purl. Sew the neckband down to the inside loosely. It must be 27 cm.

BOHUS STICKNING
KNITTING TECHNIQUES

The lively colored and textured patterns produced by Bohus Stickning were not the result of unusual knitting techniques. Rather, they reflect a keen sense of color and design experimentation on the part of the designers. The majority of the patterns were created on stockinette stitch backgrounds with interspersed purl stitches for texture.

The colorful patterning is often compared to garments worked in the Fair Isle tradition. In actuality though, there are very few similarities in terms of construction, knitting style, and color use. Fair Isle knitting is worked circularly in stockinette stitch, has just two colors per row, and utilizes steeks (a narrow section of waste stitches which are cut through when the knitting is completed) to open the knitted tube. In contrast, Bohus knitting can be worked either flat or in the round depending on the garment, includes purl stitches on a stockinette stitch background, can have any number of colors in a row, and does not use steeks.

Misinformation printed in *Odham's Encyclopedia of Knitting* by James Norbury and Margaret Agutter has lead to the belief that slip stitches were incorporated into Bohus Stickning designs. Norbury wrote, "On the outskirts of Gôteborg [sic] is the Bohus country where peasant knitters have developed a type of colour [sic] knitting peculiar to the small area they inhabit. In this type of knitting embossed effects are obtained by working some of the stitches in reverse stocking stitch on a stocking stitch background. Another element in Bohus designs is their clever use of slip stitches to build up multi-colour [sic] effects in the finished fabrics."

When Elizabeth Zimmerman introduced American knitters to Bohus Stickning in 1983, she based her comments about the unknown knitting style on this statement. Unfortunately, with so little information about Bohus Stickning available, it was not possible to confirm the authors' claim. It was reasonable to assume that slip stitches were used to bring color up from the row below, thus reducing the number of yarns carried in a row—an appealing consideration to American knitters who generally don't like to work with more than two colors in a row. However, the Bohus knitters carried as many colors in a row as the designers specified (I've seen as many as five colors in a row), without utilizing slip stitches.

In general, the techniques discussed in this chapter are those used in the original Bohus Stickning garments. However, there are a few techniques which were not specified in the original patterns, such as the method of casting on and of making increases. Knitters probably used a technique taught in the knitting classes sponsored by Bohus Stickning. Appropriate options for these unspecified techniques are given in this chapter.

A variety of methods could be substituted for a technique without affecting the wear or beauty of the garment. For example, even though the original instructions specified that the side seams be joined together with a backstitch, another seaming method can be successfully substituted.

SWEATER CONSTRUCTION AND PATTERN PLACEMENT

Bohus Stickning garments were worked in a variety of ways—from the bottom up, from the neck down, and sideways—depending on the sweater style. With the exception of the jacket that was worked sideways, all of the sweater designs—with yokes, inset yokes, and yokeless—were made into pullovers as well as cardigans.

Early designs, such as "The Red Edge", and drop shoulder designs, such as "The Zebra", were worked from the bottom up. These designs generally had patterned fronts and plain-color backs, sleeves, and ribbing. In the late 1940s, yoke designs were added to the product line. These garments were worked in "old round knitting", that is, they were worked from the neck down. The yoke designs radiated outward from the neck ribbing for approximately eight inches. The rest of the sweater was worked in a plain color. Also in the late 1940s, inset-yoke or "new round knitting" designs were created. This sweater style was knit from

the bottom up with a scoop neck. Then stitches were picked up around the scoop neck edge and knit circularly to fill in the yoke, which was approximately three inches deep. Like the other yoke sweaters, the pattern was generally limited to the area just below the neck ribbing. The jacket design incorporated pieces that were knit sideways. The patterned jacket fronts were worked from the center front buttonbands to the underarm side seams. The back and sleeves had no patterning and were worked from the bottom up.

Knitting instructions for all but the inset-yoke sweaters are included in this book.

CIRCULAR AND FLAT KNITTING

Bohus Stickning garments were knitted both flat (back and forth on straight needles) and circularly or in the round (tubular on circular or double-pointed needles). In general, color patterns are easiest if worked circularly so that the right side of the pattern always faces the knitter. But knitting was not always made easy for the Bohus knitters. Items such as tams were knit in the round, but others, such as scarves and cardigans, were always worked back and forth. Yoke and inset-yoke pullovers were worked with a combination of flat and circular knitting. The first few inches of pullovers with neckline openings were worked back and forth. Then the work was joined and the remainder of the yoke was knit in the round. The sleeves and bodies of yoke pullovers and cardigans were worked flat. Although pullover sweaters could have been easily worked in the round, as could yoke cardigans if a steek were worked at the center front, Bohus Stickning believed that side seams gave the sweaters a more refined, finished look.

For simplicity, instructions for the yoke garments included in this book are given for working entirely in the round. The sweater patterns in Chapter 4 have been updated for a contemporary fit and have more ease than the "sweater-girl" fit of the original Bohus Stickning patterns. The updated sweaters do not have keyhole openings in the back as did the sweaters of the 1940s and 1950s, and consequently, the entire yoke can be worked in the round for a pullover.

COLOR KNITTING

Color knitting is easiest worked with only two colors in a row which allows the knitter to hold one color in each hand, using the English method to knit with one and the German or Continental method to knit with the other. Unfortunately for the knitters, most of the Bohus Stickning designers did not consider this when they developed their patterns, some of which called for as many as five colors of yarns in a single row. If you select a design that has more than two colors in a row, be aware that your progress will be slower and your tension may be affected by the extra strands of yarn being carried across the back of the work.

The designers did not instruct the knitters to "catch" yarns that were carried across the back for more than one inch; the fine gauge of the knitting and the cohesive properties of the wool and angora-blend yarns tended to "hold" the strands in place. However, the knitters had to take care to keep the tension even among the stranded yarns to achieve a garment that had neither puckers from being stranded too tightly nor holes from being stranded too loosely.

GAUGE

Careful attention needs to be paid to gauge because most Bohus Stickning garments contain areas of plain stockinette stitch as well as areas of color patterning. It is crucial that the two areas have the same gauge. If they differ, parts of the finished garment will either pull in or flare out, distorting the shape of the sweater. For example, if the gauge is too tight over the color knitting in the yoke of a pullover, then the neckline will be too small and the yoke will draw in compared to the body of the sweater. Even experienced Bohus knitters had trouble with gauge at times, and many faulty sweaters were cut into sample swatches.

If you plan to make a pattern with areas of plain and areas of color knitting, you'll need to make two swatches, each at least four inches square, to determine the different gauges. Use the yarns, needles, pattern, and knitting method (either flat or circular) you intend to use in the actual garment. For example, if you plan to make a yoke pullover with the yoke worked in the round and the body and sleeves worked flat, work the swatch for the yoke circularly and the swatch for the body flat.

To work a circular swatch, use four or five double-pointed needles or a short (11") circular needle, and work a small tube with a four-inch diameter. Or you can use two double-pointed needles or a circular needle, work the first row, cut the yarns at the end of the row, do not turn, slide the stitches to the other end of the needle, and work the second row. Continue in this manner, always working with the knit side facing you, until the swatch is the desired length.

Lay the patterned and plain swatches on a flat surface. Place a pin about one-half inch from the left edge. With a tape measure or ruler, measure over three inches and place another pin. Count the number of stitches between the pins, including half and quarter stitches. This is the number of stitches in three inches of knitting. Divide this number by three to determine the number of stitches per inch. Experiment with different needle sizes until the two swatches have the same gauges. Do not be alarmed if your gauge is different for a color-patterned swatch than for a plain swatch. Knitters commonly have different gauges when working with color patterning. You can compensate for this discrepancy by using different size needles to work the yoke and the body. First, determine which of the swatches has the correct gauge. Then alter the needle size used on the swatch that is off gauge. If the gauge is too tight, that is, has more stitches per inch than desired, try a larger size needle. If the gauge of the swatch that needs adjusting is too loose, that is, has fewer stitches per inch than desired, try a smaller needle size.

CASTING ON

No specific cast-on instructions were given to the Bohus Stickning knitters. Any technique that provided an elastic edge was acceptable.

For yoke sweaters that have a ribbed neck edge that turns under, you can use whatever cast-on method you like, but I suggest that you use the Looping Provisional Cast On (from *The Handknitter's Handbook* by Montse Stanley, pages 69–70). This method produces an edge that has excellent stretch. To work the Looping Provisional Cast On (also called the Invisible Cast On), you need one needle, a foundation yarn twice the length of the required width, and the yarn to be used in the ribbing.

Step 1. Make a slip knot at one end of the foundation yarn. Make another slip knot in the ribbing yarn. Place the slip knots on a needle held in your right hand.

Step 2. In your left hand, hold the two yarns at right angles to each other, with the foundation yarn in front. Hold the yarns in your left hand so that the ribbing yarn goes around your left index finger and the foundation yarn goes around your left thumb.

Step 3. Take the right-hand needle over and behind the ribbing yarn and over and in front of the foundation yarn, over and behind the ribbing yarn again, and then under and in front of the foundation yarn. This will make two stitches, one of which will be twisted. Repeat Step 3 until you have the desired number of stitches.

Step 4. Drop the foundation slip knot at the end of the first row and tie the two foundation ends together.

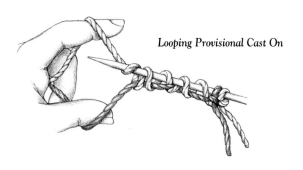

Looping Provisional Cast On

Several instructions require that stitches be added to the end of a row. An easy method is the Loop Cast On. At the end of the row where the stitches are to be added, lift the yarn onto the right needle so that it twists and then tighten the loop on the needle. Repeat this for as many stitches as are required.

Loop Cast On

GRAPHS

The increases or decreases marked on the graphs in this book indicate the exact number of stitches to be manipulated and do not require that you make adjustments as the Bohus knitters did.

Most of the Bohus Stickning designs were made by stacking several short motifs on top of one another. The motifs do not necessarily have the same number of stitches per pattern repeat. Consequently, if decreases or increases are worked in the pattern, the alignment of the patterns shifts. Although this does not cause a problem in working the designs, be aware that increases and decreases will alter pattern alignment to some extent.

INCREASES

No particular type of increase was specified in the written instructions, but knitters were instructed to use whichever increase was the "smoothest". Probably the best selection was the row-below or Lifted Increase. This increase is easy and has a clean look to it. To work the increase, knit into the stitch in the row directly below the next stitch on the needle, thereby creating the new stitch, then knit the stitch on the needle as usual.

Lifted Increase

DECREASES

None of the written instructions specify which type of decrease should be used. But examination of the original knitted items reveals that K2tog decreases were worked within areas of color patterning such as the inset yoke, and K2tog and SSK decreases were worked along armholes and sleeve caps. With the right side of the fabric facing the knitter, K2tog decreases were worked on the left-hand edges and slanted to the right, while SSK was worked on the right-hand edges and slanted to the left. Consequently, the decreases slanted together at the seam, forming subtle shaping lines.

K2tog Decrease

SSK Decrease

SHORT ROWS

On the yoke sweaters, short rows were used both for shaping and to add more length to the back of the sweater, allowing for a better fit. Short rows are incomplete rows, worked by stopping at a given point in the row, turning, and working back in the direction the row started. When a short row is turned, the stitch on the left needle, next to the turn, must be caught with the yarn to avoid leaving a hole. To do this, work to the turning point, bring the yarn to the other side of the work, slip the next stitch on the left needle to the right needle purlwise, return the yarn to the original side of the work, slip the stitch back to the left needle, turn, and work back.

Short rows were worked on the yoke sweater after the yoke pattern had been completed and the stitches had been marked for the front, back, and sleeves of the sweater. The short rows were begun at the sleeve front and worked across the back to the front of the other sleeve. For example, on a yoke cardigan, starting at the sleeve front with the body yarn, the knitter would work five stitches into the sweater front, turn (catching the sixth stitch at the turning point), purl back, purl five stitches into the opposite front, turn, knit back, knit ten stitches into the sweater front (working the wrap together with the wrapped stitch), turn, purl back, purl ten stitches into the opposite front, etc. The knitter continued to add five new sweater front stitches to each short row for the desired amount of additional shaping.

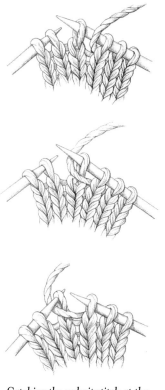

Catching the unknit stitch at the turning point of a short row. The wrap is worked together with the wrapped stitch on the following row.

BUTTON BANDS

The button bands on cardigan sweaters were knit simultaneously with the sweater, but were knit with separate balls of yarn. The button bands for the lighter weight yarns—EJA, angora, and finewool—were nine stitches wide. The button band yarn was twisted with the pattern yarns at the end of each row.

Although this method is acceptable, it tends to allow the button band to flare on the edge of a cardigan. An alternative is to work the button band separately on smaller needles and then sew it to the front edge.

Buttonholes were three stitches wide and centered on the nine-stitch-wide buttonbands. The buttonholes were made by working three stitches, binding off three stitches (the buttonhole), and working the final three stitches in the buttonband. On the next row, three stitches were cast on directly above the three bound-off stitches in the previous row.

A buttonhole method that is superior to the original method suggested is the self-reinforcing One-Row Buttonhole which can be found on pages 354–355 of *A Second Treasury of Knitting Patterns* by Barbara Walker. Work the buttonhole as follows:

Step 1. Work across the row to where you want the buttonhole to start.

Step 2. Bring the yarn to the front of the work, slip 1 stitch purlwise from the left-hand needle to the right-hand needle, pass the yarn to the back of the work, and drop it there. (The yarn is left hanging, and is not used during Steps 3 and 4.)

Step 3. Slip another stitch purlwise from the left-hand needle to the right-hand needle and pass the first stitch over it. This will bind off the first stitch. Repeat Step 3 two more times.

Step 4. Slip the last stitch back to left-hand needle and turn work.

Step 5. Pick up the hanging yarn and pass it to the back. Use the Cable Cast On as follows: *insert the right-hand needle between the first and second stitches on the left-hand needle as if to knit, catch the yarn with the needle and draw through a loop; slip this

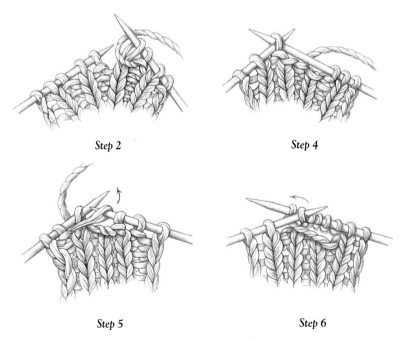

Step 2   *Step 4*

Step 5   *Step 6*

One-Row Buttonhole

loop onto the left-hand needle to serve as a new first stitch; repeat from * until four stitches have been cast on. Before placing the last loop on left-hand needle, bring the yarn through to the front, forming a dividing strand between the last stitch and the next-to-last one. Turn work again.

Step 6. Slip the first stitch from left-hand needle to right-hand needle and then pass the fourth cast-on st over it. Work to the end of the row.

BINDING OFF

In the original Bohus Stickning patterns, all of the garment pieces were simply bound off and the sweaters were assembled by sewing the shoulder, sleeve, and underarm seams, and then the sleeves were set into the armholes. You can eliminate the need to sew some seams if you bind off the shoulder seams together and bind off the sleeve into the armhole.

To bind off the shoulder seams together, place the front and back shoulder stitches onto two separate needles. Hold them together in your left hand with the right sides of the knitting facing together. In your right hand, take another needle and insert the right-hand needle into the first stitch on each of the left-hand needles and knit them as one stitch. Knit the next stitch in the same way. You now have two stitches on the right-hand needle. Pass the first stitch over the second stitch. Repeat until only one stitch remains on the right-hand needle. Cut the yarn and pull the tail through the last stitch.

To bind off the sleeve stitches into the armhole of a sweater (excluding the jacket in which the front is worked sideways), first sew the front and back together at the shoulder seams (or bind them off together, if you wish). Divide the sleeve stitches into four equal sections and mark the sections on the needle with three loops of thread or safety pins. Also divide the armhole into four equal sections marked with loops of thread or safety pins. As you work, match these markers to help ensure an even distribution of the sleeve stitches into the armhole. Begin binding off by holding the pieces in your left hand with right sides together, with the needle holding the sleeve stitches on top. Insert the right-hand needle into the first stitch on the left-hand needle and into the selvedge edge of the armhole. Knit these as one stitch.

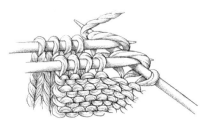

Binding off shoulder seams together.

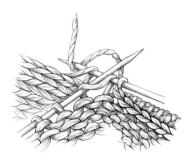

Binding off sleeve stitches into armhole.

Knit the next stitch in the same way. There will be two stitches on the right-hand needle. Pass the first stitch over the second stitch. Repeat until only one stitch remains on the right-hand needle. Cut the yarn and pull the tail through the last stitch. Then sew the sleeve and side seams as usual.

SEAMS

Seams were joined with a backstitch worked two stitches in from the edge. To prevent a gap from forming at the beginning of the seam, a figure-eight was worked at the lower edge of the knitted pieces. The figure-eight was worked by laying the pieces together on a table, right side up, inserting the needle from behind the fabric, two stitches in on the lower right edge, pulling the extra yarn through, bringing needle to the lower left edge, inserting it from behind (two stitches in from the edge), and pulling the yarn through. In some cases, the figure eight was repeated for a firmer lower seam edge.

The remainder of the seam was joined with a backstitch. The right sides of the fabric were placed together, the needle inserted from the back, up between the first and second rows, and the yarn pulled through. Next, the needle was inserted down between the first row and the cast-on edge, then up between the second and third rows, and pulled through. This process was repeated, with the needle going down where it first went up, and then up one row farther along the seam.

If you use the backstitch to finish the seams, I recommend that you work the seam just one stitch from the edge rather than two stitches from the edge as used by Bohus Stickning. The sweaters in this book are knit at a slightly heavier gauge than the original Bohus knitwear, and therefore produce more bulk at the seams.

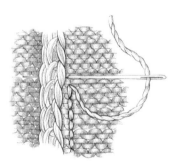

Backstitch

THE PATTERNS

The Bohus Stickning designers were adept at using a design to its fullest potential. After a design was approved, it was modified for several types of sweaters and accessories. Consequently, a customer could purchase an entire ensemble of co-ordinating garments. For example, "The Large Collar" was available in a jacket, yoke pullover, yoke cardigan, tam, scarf, and gauntlet gloves. "The Red Edge" was available in a pullover, cardigan, pixie hat, mittens, and gloves. Although the designs were versatile, no design was produced in all of the garment options available. In general, designs were either made into yoke garments (worked from the neck down) with coordinating accessories, or into pullovers and cardigans (worked from the bottom up), also with matching accessories.

Sixteen original Bohus designs are featured in this book, as well as instructions for seven different garments—cardigan, pullover, yoke cardigan, yoke pullover, jacket, cap, and mitten. Step-by-step knitting instructions are given in this chapter for forty-six of the many design/garment possibilities. If you'd like to knit a particular design/garment combination that is not included, I encourage you to carefully study the instructions and color charts to determine if the combination you want is possible, and then make the appropriate substitutions (and adjustments, where necessary).

Every attempt has been made to emulate the original Bohus Stickning designs, and at the same time, provide the contemporary knitter with realistic projects. The yarns are a slightly heavier gauge (7 stitches per inch), the fit of the garments has been updated, and where appropriate, suggestions are given for simpler construction techniques. The instructions in this book maintain the integrity of the Bohus Stickning designs and do not present, in the words of Emma Jacobsson, "vulgar replications".

ABBREVIATIONS

BB—button band color
beg—begin(ning)(s)
BO—bind off
CC—contrast color
CO—cast on
dbl dec—double decrease
dec—decreas(e)(ed)(ing)
dpn—double pointed needles
inc—increas(e)(ed)(ing)
k-wise—knitwise
MC—main color
meas—measure(s)
pm—place marker

p-wise—purlwise
p2sso—pass 2 slipped sts over
rem—remain(ning)(s)
rnd—round
RS—right side
sl—slip
st(s)—stitch(es)
St st—stockinette stitch; knit on the right side; purl on the wrong side.
tog—together
work even—work in pattern without increasing or decreasing.
WS—wrong side

THE SWAN

❧ *Designed by Karin Ivarsson* ❦

THE SWAN YOKE PULLOVER

Finished Size: 40 (44, 48)" approximate bust/chest width.

Materials: Kimmet Croft Fibers' Fairy Hare (60% Rambouillet wool, 40% Angora; 1 oz. = approx. 150 yards/137 meters): 9 (10, 11) oz. Ang 5 (MC); 1 oz. #FF46 (CC); 1/2 oz. #FF1. Alice Starmore's Scottish Campion (100% pure Shetland wool; 1 oz. = approx. 150 yards/137 meters): 1/2 oz. #85 Mogit.

Gauge: 7 sts and 10 rows equal 1" over St st. Adjust needle sizes if necessary to obtain the correct gauge (see page 69).

Needle Suggestions: Size 3 for unpatterned area—16" and 29" circular, and double pointed; size 2 for patterned area—16" and 29" circular, and double pointed; size 1 for ribbing—29" circular, and double pointed.

Note: Follow graph making increases or decreases in rounds indicated. This is necessary to make the sts in the round evenly divisible by the number of sts in the pattern repeat.

YOKE: (All Sizes) With CC, smaller 16" circular needle, and using the Looping Provisional Cast On (see page 70), CO 120 sts. Place marker (pm) at beg of rnd. (The marker will be at the back of the right shoulder on the garment.) Join, being careful not to twist sts. With CC, work 2" in k1, p1 rib. (Later, the ribbing will be folded in half to the inside of the neckline, the waste yarn will be removed, and the live sts stitched in place. This allows for plenty of give in the neck.) K1 rnd, inc 24 sts evenly: 144 sts. Beg working from graph and change to 29" needles when necessary. When graph is complete, there will be 260 (280, 300) sts. Change to larger needles. Working in MC, inc 30 (38, 46) sts evenly in the next rnd: 290 (318, 346) sts. **Mark the Body and Sleeves:** Starting at the beg of the rnd, pm after: 94 (104, 114) sts for back, 51 (55, 59) sts for left sleeve, 94 (104, 114) sts for front, and 51 (55, 59) sts for right sleeve (4 markers in place). These markers indicate seam sts. Inc 1 st each side of the marker every 4th row 11 times: 378 (406, 434) sts. Leave markers in place. Break yarn. **Short Rows:** Short rows are worked to provide a better fit. They are basically used to lower the front neck and are worked back and forth in St st. Starting at beg of rnd (back of the right shoulder), sl sts of right sleeve, right front marker, and 6 sts of right front to left-hand side of needle. With RS facing, join new yarn. Keeping tail at back of work, bring yarn from back to front between needle tips, sl first st on left-hand side of needle to right-hand side, yarn back (wrapped st). K5 sts of right front, sl marker, work to 5 sts beyond last marker (5 sts of left front worked). Continue with short rows: *Yarn forward; slip next st p-wise to right-hand needle. Yarn back; turn work. Slip first st back to right-hand needle (wrapped st). WS facing, purl to last marker (right front marker); slip marker, purl to the wrapped st, purl the wrap tog with the wrapped st on the needle, p5 more sts of right front; slip next st p-wise to right-hand needle. Yarn back; turn work. Slip first st back to right-hand needle. Yarn back (wrapped st). Knit to wrapped st of left front. Knit the wrap tog with the wrapped st on the needle, then k5 more sts of left front. Rep from*. Work 5 sts further into the front sts of the sweater on each side 4 times total (40 sts = 8 short rows) ending at left front. Beg working circularly again until yoke at center front meas 8 (9, 10)" (measured straight up) or desired length from the beg of the colorwork after the ribbing. End at back of the right shoulder marker.

DIVIDE SLEEVES AND BODY: Sleeves: With larger needles and Looping Provisional Cast On, CO 2 sets of 24 (28, 32) sts for the underarms and set aside. With larger 29" circular needle, knit across 116 (126, 136) back sts, drop yarn and needle. **Join new ball of yarn and larger 16" circular needle. Knit across 73 (77, 81) sts of left sleeve, then across cast-on sts placing marker after 12th (14th, 16th) st to mark the underarm seam: 97 (105, 113) sts. Join and work even for a total of 20 rnds, ending at marker. Dec rnd: *K1, k2tog, work until 3 sts are left before marker, SSK, k1. Work 6 rnds even. Rep from* 16 (17, 18) more times: 63 (69, 75) sts rem. The sleeve is approximately 14½ (15½, 16)" long. Change to dpn when necessary. Work 6 rnds even after last dec rnd. Final dec rnd: *K1, k2tog; rep from*: 42 (46, 50) sts. Change to smaller dpn. Work k1, p1 rib for 2–3". BO in pattern. At left under-

"The Swan" yoke pullover.

arm, pick up larger 29" circular needle with yarn attached, remove the waste yarn from left underarm sts, knit up 24 (28, 32) sts; knit across 116 (126, 136) front sts, then drop yarn and needle. Rep from** for right sleeve. **Body:** At right underarm, pick up larger 29" circular needle with yarn attached, remove the waste yarn from right underarm sts, knit up 24 (28, 32) sts: 280 (308, 336) sts. Continue working in the rnd until desired length from neck rib less body rib length. Change to smaller dpn. Work k1, p1 rib for 2–3". BO in pattern.

FINISHING: Weave underarm seams. Sew in ends. Fold neck ribbing in half to inside. Remove waste yarn and stitch in place.

THE SWAN JACKET

Finished Size: 40 (44, 48)" approximate bust/chest width.

Materials: Kimmet Croft Fibers' Fairy Hare (60% Rambouillet wool, 40% Angora; 1 oz. = approx. 150 yards/137 meters): 9 (10, 11) oz. Ang 5 (MC and BB); 2 oz. #FF46; 1 oz. #FF1. Alice Starmore's Scottish Campion (100% pure Shetland wool; 1 oz. = approx. 150 yards/ 137 meters): 1 oz. #85 Mogit.
Nine 7/16" buttons.

Gauge: 7 sts and 10 rows equal 1" over St st. Adjust needle sizes if necessary to obtain the correct gauge (see page 69).

Needle Suggestions: Size 3 for unpatterned area; size 2 for patterned area; size 1 for bands.

RIGHT FRONT: With smallest needle and BB (band color) CO 154 (161, 168) sts. K6 rows. K16 sts, *work One-Row Buttonhole (see page 74), k17 (18, 19) sts, rep from* 6 times total; work One-Row Buttonhole, k15 (16, 17) sts. K5 rows (total of 6 garter st ridges). Change to medium needles and work 2 rows St st in BB color. Beg working from graph. Work even for 1½ (2, 2½)". Keeping in pattern, inc 1 st at neck edge (right side) 4 times, inc 2 sts once, inc 3 sts once, inc 5 sts once, inc 7 sts once: 175 (182, 189) sts. When graph is complete, work in MC until piece meas approximately 5¾ (6¼, 6¾)" from beg. RS facing, bind off 62 (69, 76) sts for armhole. Work 2 rows. RS facing, BO 2 sts at armhole edge 4 times: 105 sts rem (all sizes). This is the side seam and should meas approximately 15". Work even for 1". Piece should meas approximately 10½ (11, 11½)" from beg. BO rem 105 sts. With smallest needles and BB, pick up and k80 (85, 90) sts along bottom edge. K7 more rows. Next row: K74 (79, 84) sts, work One-Row Buttonhole, knit to end of row. K6 more rows. Using medium needle, BO on reverse side of knit (8 garter ridges).

LEFT FRONT: Work same as Right Front, reversing shaping and omitting buttonholes.

BACK: With largest needle and MC, CO 142 (156, 170) sts. Change to smallest needle. Work 1" in garter st. Change to largest needle. Work even in St st until piece meas 16" from beg. BO 2 sts at the beg of next 8 rows. Work until piece meas 26 (27, 28)" from beg. Place rem sts on 3 holders: 40 (44, 48) sts for each shoulder,

and 46 (52, 58) sts for back.

SLEEVES: With largest needle and MC, CO 62 (70, 80) sts. Change to smallest needle. Work 1" in garter st. Change to largest needle and St st. Inc 6 (10, 12) sts evenly across next row: 68 (80, 92) sts. Inc 1 st each side every 4th row 31 (31, 32) times and every 6th row 5 (6, 6) times: 140 (154, 168) sts. Work even until piece meas 17½ (18, 18½)" from beg. BO 2 sts beg of next 8 rows. Place rem sts on holder.

FINISHING: Join shoulder seams. With smallest needle and BB, pick up and k45 (48, 50) sts from right center front to shoulder seam, 46 (52, 58) sts from back neck holder, 45 (48, 50) sts from shoulder seam to left center front: 136 (148, 158) sts. K3 more rows (2 garter ridges). On the next row dec 13 (16, 18) sts evenly across row. K1 more row. On next row, k3, work One-Row Buttonhole, knit to end of row. K1 more row. On next row dec 6 (9, 11) sts evenly across row: 117 (123, 129) sts. K3 more rows. Using medium needle, BO on reverse side in knit. BO or sew sleeves into armhole (see page 75). Sew side and sleeve seams.

THE SWAN CAP

Finished Size: 21 (23)" circumference.
Materials: Kimmet Croft Fibers' Fairy Hare (60% Rambouillet wool, 40% Angora; 1 oz. = approx. 150 yards/137 meters): 1 oz. Ang 5 (MC); 1/2 oz. #FF46 (CC); and 1/3 oz. #FF1. Alice Starmore's Scottish Campion (100% pure Shetland wool; 1 oz. = approx.

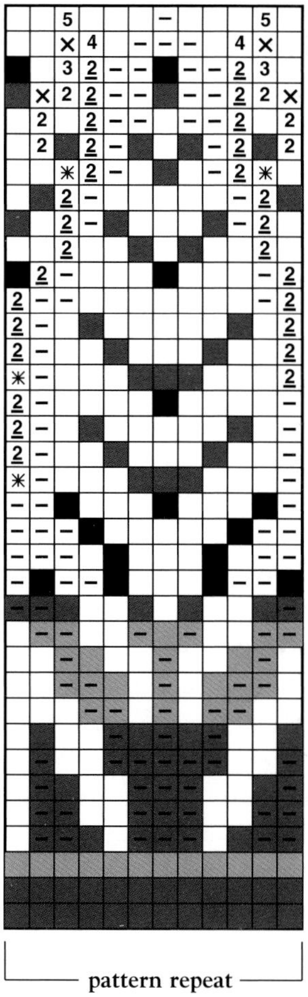
20 st rep
18 st rep
16 st rep
14 st rep
13 st rep
Rnd 3
pattern repeat

- Ang 5 (MC & BB)
- #85 Mogit
- FF46 (CC)
- FF1
- × make knit st
- 2 2 purl sts
- ✱ make purl st
- 3 2, 3, 4, or 5 knit sts
- – purl on RS, knit on WS

CAP

Work even in 12 st pattern repeat as given.

JACKET

Work even in 12 st pattern repeat as given.

PULLOVER

Rnd 3: inc 12 (24, 36) sts: 156 (168, 180) sts. Work incs as given on graph.

150 yards/137 meters): 1/4 oz. #85 Mogit.

Gauge: 7 sts and 10 rows equal 1" over St st. Adjust needle sizes if necessary to obtain the correct gauge (see page 69).

Needle Suggestions: Size 2 for patterned area—16" circular, and double pointed; size 1 for ribbing: 16" circular.

With CC and smaller needle, CO 136 (146) sts. Place marker at beg of rnd. Join, being careful not to twist sts. Work 3/4" in k1, p1 rib. Change to larger needle, work 1 rnd, inc 20 (22) sts evenly: 156 (168) sts. Follow graph, but do not work inc marked on graph. After completing graph, work even in MC until piece meas approximately 7" from beg. With MC, work 1 rnd, dec 9 (7) sts evenly spaced in rnd: 147 (161) sts. **Seven Point Crown:** Begin working with circular needles and change to dpn when necessary. Work dbl dec at seven points as follows: sl 2 sts k-wise tog, k1, p2sso. *Rnd 1:* *K18 (20), dbl dec; rep from* 6 more times. *Rnd 2 and even numbered rnds:* Knit. *Rnd 3:* *K16 (18), dbl dec; rep from* 6 more times. Continue in this manner, working 1 less st before and after each dbl dec until 21 sts rem. Work dbl dec around: 7 sts rem. Draw yarn through 7 sts. Sew in ends.

DOTS

❧ *Designed by Kerstin Olsson* ❧

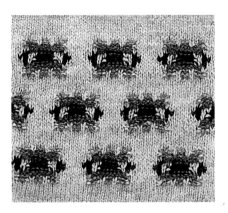

DOTS PULLOVER

Finished Size: 40 (42, 44, 46, 48)" approximate bust/chest width.

Materials: Alice Starmore's Scottish Campion (100% pure Shetland wool; 1 oz. = approx. 150 yards/137 meters): 11 (12, 12, 12, 13) skeins #93 Natural (MC); 1 skein each #89 Mooskit, #85 Mogit, #7 Black.

Gauge: 7 sts and 10 rows equal 1" over St st. Adjust needle sizes if necessary to obtain the correct gauge (see page 69).

Needle Suggestions: Size 3 for body and sleeves; size 2 for ribbing— straight and 16" circular.

BACK: With MC and smaller needles, CO 125 (133, 139, 147, 153) sts. Work k1, p1 rib for 3" ending on RS row. WS facing, purl across inc 14 sts evenly spaced: 139 (147, 153, 161, 167) sts. Change to larger needles and St st. Work even in St st until piece meas 13 1/2 (14,

14 1/2, 15, 15 1/2)" from beg. BO 2 sts at beg of next 8 rows: 123 (131, 137, 145, 151) sts rem. Work even until piece meas 23 1/2 (24 1/2, 25 1/2, 26 1/2, 27 1/2)" from beg. Divide sts onto 3 holders: 36 (39, 41, 44, 46) sts for each shoulder, and 51 (53, 55, 57, 59) sts for back neck.

FRONT: With MC and smaller needles, CO 125 (133, 139, 147, 153) sts. Work k1, p1 rib for 3" ending on RS row. WS facing, purl across inc 13 sts evenly spaced: 138 (146, 152, 160, 166) sts. Change to larger needles. Follow graph instructions. Work even in established pattern until piece meas 13 1/2 (14, 14 1/2, 15, 15 1/2)" from beg. BO 2 sts at beg of next 8 rows: 122 (130, 136, 144, 150) sts rem. Work even until piece meas 21 (22, 23, 24, 25)" from beg. **Shape neck:** Keeping in pattern, work 47 (50, 52, 55, 57) sts, place center 28 (30, 32, 34, 36) sts on holder. Attach new balls of yarn, work rem 47 (50, 52, 55, 57) sts. Keeping in pattern and working both sides at the same time, BO from each neck edge 4 sts once, 3 sts once, 2 sts once, then dec 1 st twice: 36 (39, 41, 44, 46) sts rem. Keeping in pattern, work even until piece meas 23 1/2 (24 1/2, 25 1/2, 26 1/2, 27 1/2)" from beg. Place rem shoulder sts on holder.

SLEEVES: With smaller needles and MC, CO 63 (67, 71, 75, 79) sts. Work k1, p1 rib for 3" ending on RS row. WS facing, purl across inc 7 (9, 11, 13, 15) sts evenly spaced: 70 (76, 82, 88, 94) sts. Change to larger needles and St st. Inc 1 st each side every 4th row 30 (31, 31, 31, 31) times, then every 6th row 5 (5, 5, 6, 6) times: 140 (148, 154, 162, 168) sts. Work even until sleeve meas 17 (17 1/2,

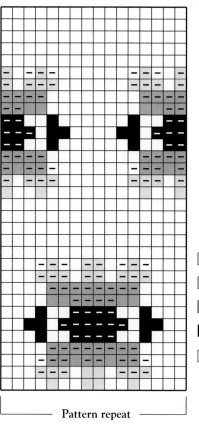

<table>
<tr><td>☐</td><td>#93 Natural (MC)</td></tr>
<tr><td>☐</td><td>#89 Mooskit</td></tr>
<tr><td>▨</td><td>#85 Mogit</td></tr>
<tr><td>■</td><td>#7 Black</td></tr>
<tr><td>−</td><td>purl on RS,
knit on WS</td></tr>
</table>

Pattern repeat

PULLOVER

With MC, k5 (1, 4, 0, 3) sts, rep graph 8 (9, 9, 10, 10) times, k5 (1, 4, 0, 3) sts.

CARDIGAN

Right Front: Beginning at center front, work pattern repeat 4 (4, 4, 5, 5) times, k8 (12, 14, 2, 6) sts with MC.

Left Front: Beginning at side edge with MC, k8 (12, 14, 2, 6) sts, work pattern repeat 4 (4, 4, 5, 5) times.

$17\frac{1}{2}$, 18, 18)" from beg. BO 2 sts at the beg of next 8 rows. Place rem 124 (132, 138, 146, 152) sts on holder.

FINISHING: BO fronts and back tog at shoulder seam (see page 75). Starting at the left shoulder seam, with MC and circular needle, pick up and knit 25 sts along left front neck edge, 28 (30, 32, 34, 36) sts from front holder, 24 sts along right neck edge, and 51 (53, 55, 57, 59) sts from back holder : 128 (132, 136, 140, 144) sts. Work k1, p1 rib for 1". BO in pattern. BO sleeves onto the body (see page 75). Sew side and sleeve seams.

DOTS CARDIGAN

Finished Size: 40 (42, 44, 46, 48)" approximate bust/chest width.

Materials: Alice Starmore's Scottish Campion (100% pure Shetland wool; 1 oz. = approx. 150 yards/137 meters): 11 (11, 12, 12, 12) skeins #93 Natural (MC); 1 skein each #89 Mooskit, #85 Mogit, #7 Black.
Seven 7/16" buttons.

Gauge: 7 sts and 10 rows equal 1" over St st. Adjust needle sizes if necessary to obtain the correct gauge (see page 69).

Needle Suggestions: Size 3 for body and sleeves; size 2 for ribbing.

BACK: With MC and smaller needles, CO 133 (141, 147, 155, 161) sts. Work k1, p1 rib for 1" ending on RS row. WS facing, purl across inc 8 sts evenly spaced: 141 (149, 155, 163, 169) sts. Change to larger needles and St st. Work even until piece meas $10\frac{1}{2}$ (11, 11, $11\frac{1}{2}$, $11\frac{1}{2}$)" from beg.

BO 2 sts at beg of next 8 rows: 125 (133, 139, 147, 153) sts rem. Work even until piece meas $20\frac{1}{2}$ ($21\frac{1}{2}$, 22, 23, $23\frac{1}{2}$)" from beg. Divide sts onto 3 holders: 38 (42, 44, 47, 49) sts for each shoulder, and 49 (49, 51, 53, 55) sts for back neck.

RIGHT FRONT: With MC and smaller needles, CO 75 (79, 81, 85, 89) sts. Work k1, p1 rib for 1/2". With RS facing, rib 2 sts, work the One-Row Buttonhole (see page 74), rib to end. Work an additional 1/2" of k1, p1 rib, ending on RS row. WS facing, purl across inc 4 sts evenly spaced, maintain rib over last 7 sts: 79 (83, 85, 89, 93) sts. With RS facing, rib 7 sts and place on holder (Buttonhole Band): 72 (76, 78, 82, 86) sts rem. Change to larger needles and St st. At the same time, follow graph instructions. Work even until piece meas $10\frac{1}{2}$ (11, 11, $11\frac{1}{2}$, $11\frac{1}{2}$)" from beg ending with a RS row. With WS facing, BO 2 sts at armhole edge 4 times: 64 (68, 70, 74, 78) sts rem. Work even until piece meas 18 (19, $19\frac{1}{2}$, $20\frac{1}{2}$, 21)" from beg ending with a WS row. **Shape neck:** At neck edge, keeping in pattern, BO 14 (14, 14, 15, 17) sts once, 4 sts once, 2 sts twice, then dec 1 st every other row 4 times: 38 (42, 44, 47, 49) sts rem. Keeping in pattern, work even until piece meas $20\frac{1}{2}$ ($21\frac{1}{2}$, 22, 23, $23\frac{1}{2}$)" from beg. Place rem shoulder sts on holder.

LEFT FRONT: Work as for Right Front reversing shaping and omitting buttonhole in bottom ribbing.

SLEEVES: With smaller needles and MC, CO 63 (67, 71, 75, 79) sts. Work k1, p1 rib for 1" ending on RS row. WS facing, purl across inc 7 (9, 11, 13, 15) sts

evenly spaced: 70 (76, 82, 88, 94) sts. Change to larger needles and St st. Inc 1 st each side every 4th row 30 (31, 31, 31, 31) times, then every 6th row 5 (5, 5, 6, 6) times: 140 (148, 154, 162, 168) sts. Work even until sleeve meas 17 ($17\frac{1}{2}$, $17\frac{1}{2}$, 18, 18)" from beg. BO 2 sts at the beg of next 8 rows. Place rem 124 (132, 138, 146, 152) sts on holder.

BUTTON BANDS: Right: With smaller needles and MC, pick up the 7 sts of right Buttonhole Band from holder. *Work even in k1, p1 rib for approximately $2\frac{3}{4}$ (3, 3, $3\frac{1}{4}$, $3\frac{1}{3}$)" from last buttonhole. With RS facing, rib 2 sts, work the One-Row Buttonhole, rib to end. Rep from* 4 more times. Continue in k1, p1 rib for $2\frac{1}{4}$ ($2\frac{1}{2}$, $2\frac{1}{2}$, $2\frac{3}{4}$, $2\frac{3}{4}$)". Do not break yarn. Place sts on holder. The last buttonhole will be made in the neckband. **Left:** Rep as for right Button Band, omitting buttonholes and breaking yarn.

FINISHING: BO fronts and back tog at shoulder seam (see page 75). With smaller needles, RS facing and MC attached, rib 7 sts of right Buttonhole Band from holder, pick up and knit 35 (35, 37, 37, 39) sts along right neck edge, 49 (49, 51, 53, 55) sts from back holder, 35 (35, 37, 37, 39) sts along left neck edge, rib 7 sts of left Button Band from holder: 133 (133, 139, 141, 147) sts. Work k1, p1 rib for 1/2", work the One-Row Buttonhole at neckline on right front band. Work an additional 1/2" of k1, p1 rib. BO in pattern. Sew Button Bands to center front edges. BO sleeves onto the body (see page 75). Sew side and sleeve seams. Sew on buttons.

"The Red Edge" cardigan.

THE RED EDGE

❖ Designed by
Anna-Lisa Mannheimer Lunn ❖

THE RED EDGE PULLOVER

Finished Size: 40 (42, 44, 46, 48)" approximate bust/chest width.

Materials: Alice Starmore's Scottish Campion (100% pure Shetland wool; 1 oz. = approx. 150 yards/137 meters): 9 (9, 10, 10, 11) skeins #93 Natural (MC); 1 skein each #85 Mogit, #134 Shaela, #127 Sage, #90 Moss, #152 Teal, #22 Chartreuse, #98 Ochre, #18 Burnt Umber, #7 Black, #23 Chestnut, #102 Pale Green.

Gauge: 7 sts and 10 rows equal 1" over St st. Adjust needle sizes if necessary to obtain the correct gauge (see page 69).

Needle Suggestions: Size 3 for body and sleeves; size 2 for ribbing—straight and 16" circular.

BACK: With MC and smaller needles, CO 125 (133, 139, 147, 153) sts. Work k1, p1 rib for 3" ending on RS row. WS facing, purl across inc 14 sts evenly spaced: 139 (147, 153, 161, 167) sts. Change to larger needles and St st. Work even in St st until piece meas 13½ (14, 14½, 15, 15½)" from beg. BO 2 sts at beg of next 8 rows: 123 (131, 137, 145, 151) sts rem. Work even until piece meas 23½ (24½, 25½, 26½, 27½)" from beg. Divide sts onto 3 holders: 36 (39, 41, 44, 46) sts for each shoulder, and 51 (53, 55, 57, 59) sts for back neck.

FRONT: With MC and smaller nee-

dles, CO 125 (133, 139, 147, 153) sts. Work k1, p1 rib for 3" ending on RS row. WS facing, purl across inc 13 sts evenly spaced: 138 (146, 152, 160, 166) sts. Change to larger needles. With MC, follow graph instructions. Work even in established pattern until piece meas 13½ (14, 14½, 15, 15½)" from beg. BO 2 sts at beg of next 8 rows: 122 (130, 136, 144, 150) sts rem. Work even until piece meas 21 (22, 23, 24, 25)" from beg. **Shape neck:** Keeping in pattern, work 47 (50, 52, 55, 57) sts, place center 28 (30, 32, 34, 36) sts on holder. Attach new balls of yarn, work rem 47 (50, 53, 55, 57) sts. Keeping in pattern and working both sides at the same time, BO from each neck edge 4 sts once, 3 sts once, 2 sts once, then dec 1 st twice: 36 (39, 41, 44, 46) sts rem. Keeping in pattern, work even until piece meas 23½ (24½, 25½, 26½, 27½)" from beg. Place rem shoulder sts on holder.

SLEEVES: With smaller needles and MC, CO 63 (67, 71, 75, 79) sts. Work k1, p1 rib for 3" ending on RS row. WS facing, purl across inc 7 (9, 11, 13, 15) sts evenly spaced: 70 (76, 82, 88, 94) sts. Change to larger needles and St st. Inc 1 st each side every 4th row 30 (31, 31, 31, 31) times, then every 6th row 5 (5, 5, 6, 6) times: 140 (148, 154, 162, 168) sts. Work even until sleeve meas 17 (17½, 17½, 18, 18)" from beg. BO 2 sts at the beg of next 8 rows. Place rem 124 (132, 138, 146, 152) sts on holder.

FINISHING: BO fronts and back tog at shoulder seam (see page 75). Starting at the left shoulder seam, with MC and circular needle, pick up and knit 25 sts

along left front neck edge, 28 (30, 32, 34, 36) sts from front holder, 24 sts along right neck edge, and 51 (53, 55, 57, 59) sts from back holder: 128 (132, 136, 140, 144) sts. Work k1, p1 rib for 1". BO in pattern. BO sleeves onto the body (see page 75). Sew side and sleeve seams.

THE RED EDGE CARDIGAN

Finished Size: 40 (42, 44, 46, 48)" approximate bust/chest width.

Materials: Alice Starmore's Scottish Campion (100% pure Shetland wool; 1 oz. = approx. 150 yards/137 meters): 9 (9, 10, 10, 11) skeins #93 Natural (MC); 1 skein each #85 Mogit, #134 Shaela, #127 Sage, #90 Moss, #152 Teal, #22 Chartreuse, #98 Ochre, #18 Burnt Umber, #7 Black, #23 Chestnut, #102 Pale Green.
Seven 7/16" buttons.

Gauge: 7 sts and 10 rows equal 1" over St st. Adjust needle sizes if necessary to obtain the correct gauge (see page 69).

Needle Suggestions: Size 3 for body and sleeves; size 2 for ribbing.

BACK: With MC and smaller needles, CO 133 (141, 147, 155, 161) sts. Work k1, p1 rib for 1". Change to larger needles and St st. Inc 1 st each side every 1", 4 times: 141 (149, 155, 163, 169) sts. Work even until piece meas 10½ (11, 11, 11½, 11½)" from beg. BO 2 sts at beg of next 8 rows: 125 (133, 139, 147, 153) sts rem. Work even until piece meas 20½ (21½, 22, 23, 23½)" from beg. Divide sts onto 3 holders: 38 (42, 44, 47, 49) sts for

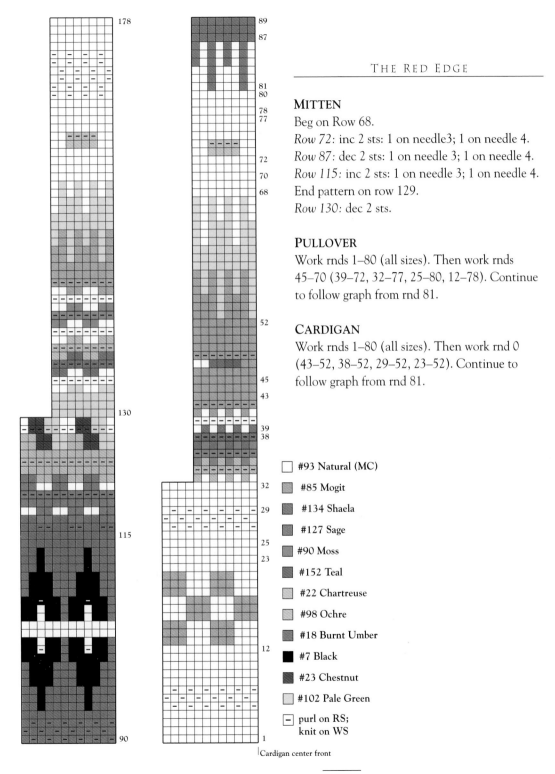

MITTEN

Beg on Row 68.

Row 72: inc 2 sts: 1 on needle3; 1 on needle 4.

Row 87: dec 2 sts: 1 on needle 3; 1 on needle 4.

Row 115: inc 2 sts: 1 on needle 3; 1 on needle 4.

End pattern on row 129.

Row 130: dec 2 sts.

PULLOVER

Work rnds 1–80 (all sizes). Then work rnds 45–70 (39–72, 32–77, 25–80, 12–78). Continue to follow graph from rnd 81.

CARDIGAN

Work rnds 1–80 (all sizes). Then work rnd 0 (43–52, 38–52, 29–52, 23–52). Continue to follow graph from rnd 81.

☐ #93 Natural (MC)

▨ #85 Mogit

▨ #134 Shaela

▨ #127 Sage

▨ #90 Moss

▨ #152 Teal

▨ #22 Chartreuse

▨ #98 Ochre

▨ #18 Burnt Umber

■ #7 Black

▨ #23 Chestnut

▨ #102 Pale Green

⊟ purl on RS;
knit on WS

Cardigan center front

each shoulder, and 49 (49, 51, 53, 55) sts for back neck.

RIGHT FRONT: With MC and smaller needles, CO 75 (79, 81, 85, 89) sts. Work k1, p1 rib for 1/2". With RS facing, rib 2 sts, work the One-Row Buttonhole (see page 74), rib to end. Work even in rib for 1/2". With RS facing, rib 7 sts and place on holder (Buttonhole Band): 68 (72, 74, 78, 82) sts rem. Change to larger needles and St st. Follow graph instructions and at the same time, inc 1 st at side seam every 1", 4 times: 72, (76, 78, 82, 86) sts. Work even until piece meas 10½ (11, 11, 11½, 11½)" from beg ending with a RS row. With WS facing, BO 2 sts at armhole edge 4 times: 64 (68, 70, 74, 78) sts rem. Work even until piece meas 18 (19, 19½, 20½, 21)" from beg ending with a WS row. **Shape neck:** At neck edge, keeping in pattern, BO 14 (14, 14, 15, 17) once, 4 sts once, 2 sts twice, then dec 1 st every other row 4 times: 38 (42, 44, 47, 49) sts rem. Keeping in pattern, work even until piece meas 20½ (21½, 22, 23, 23½)" from beg. Place rem shoulder sts on holder.

LEFT FRONT: Beg on WS row. Work as for Right Front reversing shaping and omitting buttonhole in bottom ribbing.

SLEEVES: With smaller needles and MC, CO 63 (67, 71, 75, 79) sts. Work k1, p1 rib for 1" ending on RS row. WS facing, purl across inc 7 (9, 11, 13, 15) evenly: 70 (76, 82, 88, 94) sts. Change to larger needles and St st. Inc 1 st each side every 4th row 30 (31, 31, 31, 31) times, then every 6th row 5 (5, 5, 6, 6) times: 140 (148, 154, 162, 168) sts. Work even until sleeve meas 17 (17½, 17½, 18, 18)"

from beg. BO 2 sts at the beg of next 8 rows. Place rem 124 (132, 138, 146, 152) sts on holder.

BUTTON BANDS: Right: With smaller needles and MC, pick up the 7 sts of right Buttonhole Band from holder. *Work even in k1, p1 rib for approximately 2¾ (3, 3, 3¼, 3⅓)" from last buttonhole. With RS facing, rib 2 sts, work the One-Row Buttonhole, rib to end. Rep from* 4 more times. Continue in k1, p1 rib for 2¼ (2½, 2½, 2¾, 2¾)". Do not break yarn. Place sts on holder. The last buttonhole will be made in the neckband. **Left:** Rep as for right Button Band, omitting buttonholes and breaking yarn.

FINISHING: BO fronts and back tog at shoulder seam (see page 75). With smaller needles, RS facing, and MC attached, rib 7 sts of right Buttonhole Band from holder, pick up and knit 35 (35, 37, 37, 39) sts along right neck edge, 49 (49, 51, 53, 55) sts from back holder, 35 (35, 37, 37, 39) sts along left neck edge, rib 7 sts of left Button Band from holder: 133 (133, 139, 141, 147) sts. Work k1, p1 rib for 1/2", work the One-Row Buttonhole at neckline on right front band. Work an additional 1/2" of k1, p1 rib. BO in pattern. Sew Button Bands to center front edges. BO sleeves onto the body (see page 75). Sew side and sleeve seams. Sew on buttons.

THE RED EDGE MITTENS

Size: Women's.

Materials: Alice Starmore's Scottish Campion (100% pure Shetland wool;

1 oz. = approx. 150 yards/137 meters): 1 oz. #93 Natural (MC); 1/4 oz. each #18 Burnt Umber, #22 Chartreuse, #7 Black, #152 Teal, #98 Ochre, #127 Sage, #23 Chestnut.

Gauge: 7 sts and 10 rows equal 1" over St st. Adjust needle sizes if necessary to obtain the correct gauge.

Needle Suggestions: Size 2 double pointed (set of five).

CUFF: (Select desired style.) **Reverse St st cuff:** With MC, CO 60 sts. Divide evenly between 4 needles (15 sts per needle). Join, being careful not to twist sts. Work even in St st for 2½". Turn cuff inside out, so the reverse St st becomes the right side. The needle where the yarn end is located is needle 1. The other needles are numbered clockwise from needle 1. With yarn in back, slip one st from needle 4 to needle 1, bring yarn forward, slip st back to needle 4. You have worked a turn st which will prevent a hole in the cuff. Work one rnd in St st, dec 6 sts evenly at the same time. Work one rnd even. Work one more rnd, inc 6 sts evenly: 60 sts. Continue at Mitten Body. **Rib cuff:** With MC, CO 54 sts. Divide between 4 needles (13, 14, 13, 14 sts per needle). Join, being careful not to twist sts. Work in k1, p1 rib for 3". Work one rnd in St st inc 6 sts evenly: 60 sts. Continue at Mitten Body. **Note:** 1. Needles 1 and 2 hold the palm sts for the mitten and are worked in MC. Needles 3 and 4 hold the patterned, back side of the mitten and are worked in multiple colors following graph. 2. Follow graph making increases or decreases in rnds indicated. This is necessary to make the sts in the rnd evenly divisible by the number of sts in the pattern repeat. 3. The cuff and mitten top are worked in the rnd in MC. The patterned portion of the mitten is worked back and forth in St st in multiple colors (see Mitten Body).

MITTEN BODY: Right Hand: Starting with needle 1, k1, p1, k3, place marker, p1, k9. Knit across needle 2. Leave yarn at the end of needle 2. Go to needle 4 and attach a second ball of MC. Turn work. Purl across needles 4 and 3. Twist the yarn ends between needles 2 and 3 to close the side of the mitten. The patterned side of the mitten will be facing you. Work Row 1 of chart. Purl across needles 2 and 1. Twist the yarn ends between needles 1 and 4 to close the other side of the mitten. The palm of the mitten is always worked in MC. Continue working back and forth, twisting the yarn at row ends. At the same time, on the palm side work a thumb gusset by inc 1 st every knit row before the marker, 12 times. After the final thumb gusset inc row, twist yarns at end of row and purl back to marker. Place 17 sts after marker on a holder. CO 6 sts at end of purl row: 15 sts on needle 1. Work even in St st until graph is completed. **Shape Mitten Top:** With MC and starting at needle 1, k2 rnds. *K1, SSK, knit to last 3 sts on needle 2, k2tog, k1. Then, k1, SSK, knit to last 3 sts on needle 4, k2tog, K1. Rep from* until 8 sts rem. Draw yarn through sts and tighten to end off. **Thumb:** Put 17 sts on holder onto one dpn. Knit across 8 sts on needle 1, knit across next 8 sts for needle 2, knit rem st onto needle 3 and pick up and knit 7 sts along the CO

sts. There will be a total of 24 sts, 8 per needle. Working in the rnd, work even in St st for 28 rnds. In the next rnd, k2tog across rnd: 12 sts rem. In the next rnd, k2tog across rnd: 6 sts rem. Draw yarn through sts and tighten to end off. **Left Hand:** After the cuff is worked, knit across needle 1, k9 sts on needle 2, p1, place marker, k3, p1, k1. Continue to work the same as Right Hand.

FINISHING: Sew in ends. For the reverse St st cuff, if desired, brush cuff with a stiff brush (such as a vegetable brush) to raise the nap.

DEAN

❧ *Designed by*
Anna-Lisa Mannheimer Lunn ❧

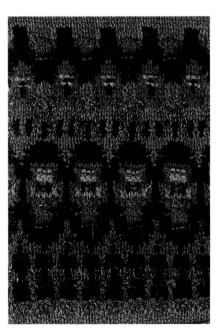

Finished Size: 40 (44, 48)" approximate bust/chest width.

Materials: Kimmet Croft Fibers' Fairy Hare (60% Rambouillet wool, 40% Angora; 1 oz. = approx. 150 yards/137 meters): 8 (9, 10) oz. #FF1 (MC); 1/2 oz. each #FF82, and #FF70; 1/3 oz #FF78; 1/4 oz. each #FF72, #FF66, #FF64, and #FF81. Jamieson & Smith's 2 Ply Jumper Weight (100% pure Shetland wool; 1 oz. = approx. 150 yards/137 meters): 1/3 oz. #203 Silver Gray.

Gauge: 7 sts and 10 rows equal 1" over St st. Adjust needle sizes if necessary to obtain the correct gauge (see page 69).

Needle Suggestions: Size 3 for unpatterned area—16" and 29" circular, and double pointed; size 2 for patterned area—16" and 29" circular, and double pointed; size 1 for ribbing—29" circular, and double pointed.

Note: Follow graph making increases or decreases in rounds indicated. This is necessary to make the sts in the round evenly divisible by the number of sts in the pattern repeat.

YOKE: (All Sizes) With MC, smaller 16" circular needle, and using the Looping Provisional Cast On (see page 70), CO 120 sts. Place marker (pm) at beg of rnd. (The marker will be at the back of the right shoulder on the garment.) Join, being careful not to twist sts. With MC, work 2" in k1, p1 rib. (Later, the ribbing will be folded in half to the inside of the neckline, the waste yarn removed and the live sts stitched in place. This allows for

CAP AND JACKET
Work even in pattern repeat as given.

PULLOVER AND CARDIGAN
Rnd 8: inc 72 sts: 216 sts
Rnd 25: inc 72 (88, 112) sts: 288 (304, 328) sts.
Rnd 51: inc 88 (96, 104) sts: 376 (400, 432) sts.

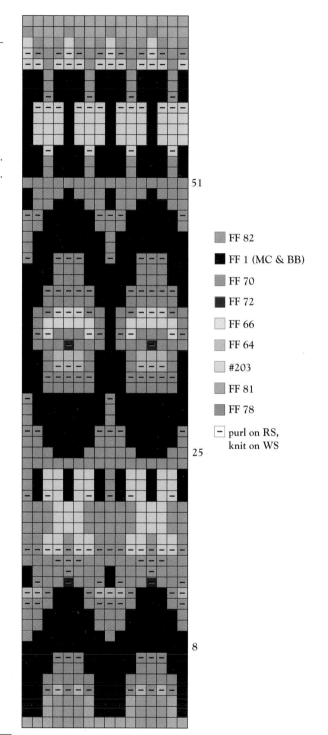

▨	FF 82
■	FF 1 (MC & BB)
▨	FF 70
▨	FF 72
☐	FF 66
▨	FF 64
☐	#203
▨	FF 81
▨	FF 78
−	purl on RS, knit on WS

plenty of give in the neck.) K1 rnd MC, inc 24 sts evenly: 144 sts. Beg working from graph and change to 29" needles when necessary. When graph is complete, work in MC and inc 2 (6, 2) sts in first plain rnd: 378 (406, 434) sts. Change to larger needles. **Mark the Body and Sleeves:** Starting at the beg of the rnd, pm after: 116 (126, 136) sts for back, 73 (77, 81) sts for left sleeve, 116 (126, 136) sts for front, and 73 (77, 81) sts for right sleeve (4 markers in place). Break yarn.

Short Rows: Short rows are worked to provide a better fit. They are basically used to lower the front neck and are worked back and forth in St st. Starting at beg of rnd (back of the right shoulder), sl sts of right sleeve, right front marker and 6 sts of right front to left-hand side of needle. With RS facing, join new yarn. Keeping tail at back of work, bring yarn from back to front between needle tips, sl first st on left-hand side of needle to right-hand side, yarn back (wrapped st). K5 sts of right front, sl marker, work to 5 sts beyond last marker (5 sts of left front worked). Continue with short rows: *Yarn forward; slip next st p-wise to right-hand needle. Yarn back; turn work. Slip first st back to right-hand needle (wrapped st). WS facing, purl to last marker (right front marker); slip marker, purl to the wrapped st, purl the wrap tog with the wrapped st on the needle, p5 more sts of right front; slip next st p-wise to right-hand needle. Yarn back; turn work. Slip first st back to right-hand needle. Yarn back (wrapped st). Knit to wrapped st of left front. Knit the wrap tog with the wrapped st on the needle, then k5 more sts of left front. Rep from*. Work

5 sts further into the front sts of the sweater on each side 4 times total (40 sts = 8 short rows) ending at left front. Beg working circularly again until yoke at center front meas 8 (9, 10)" (measured straight up) or desired length from the beg of the colorwork after the ribbing. End at back of the right shoulder marker.

DIVIDE SLEEVES AND BODY: Sleeves: With larger needles and Looping Provisional Cast On, CO 2 sets of 24 (28, 32) sts for underarms and set aside. With larger 29" circular needle, knit across 116 (126, 136) back sts, drop yarn and needle. **Join new ball of yarn and larger 16" circular needle. Knit across 73 (77, 81) sts of left sleeve, then across cast-on sts placing marker after 12th (14th, 16th) st: 97 (105, 113) sts. Join and work even for a total of 20 rnds, ending at marker. Dec rnd: *K1, k2tog, work until 3 sts are left before marker, SSK, k1. Work 6 rnds even. Rep from* 16 (17, 18) more times: 63 (69, 75) sts rem. The sleeve is approximately 14½ (15¼, 16)" long. Change to dpn when necessary. Work 6 rnds even after last dec rnd. Final dec rnd: *K1, k2tog; rep from*: 42 (46, 50) sts rem. Change to smaller dpn. Work k1, p1 rib for 2–3". BO in pattern. At left underarm, pick up larger 29" circular needle with yarn attached, remove the waste yarn from left underarm sts, knit up 24 (28, 32) sts; knit across 116 (126, 136) front sts, then drop yarn and needle. Rep from** for right sleeve. **Body:** At right underarm, pick up larger 29" circular needle with yarn attached, remove the waste yarn from right underarm sts, knit up 24 (28, 32) sts: 280 (308, 336) sts. Contin-

ue working in the rnd until desired length from neck rib less body rib length. Change to smaller dpn. Work in k1, p1 rib for 2–3". BO in pattern.

Finishing: Weave underarm seams. Sew in ends. Fold neck ribbing in half to inside. Remove waste yarn and stitch in place.

DEAN YOKE CARDIGAN

Finished Size: 40 (44, 48)" approximate bust/chest width.

Materials: Kimmet Croft Fibers' Fairy Hare (60% Rambouillet wool, 40% Angora; 1 oz. = approx. 150 yards/137 meters): 8 (9, 10) oz. #FF1 (MC); 1/2 oz. each #FF82, and #FF70; 1/4 oz. each #FF72, #FF66, #FF64, and #FF81; and 1/3 oz #FF78. Jamieson & Smith's 2 Ply Jumper Weight (100% pure Shetland wool; 1 oz. = approx. 150 yards/137 meters): 1/3 oz. #203 Silver Gray.
Nine 5/8" buttons.

Gauge: 7 sts and 10 rows equal 1" over St st. Adjust needle sizes if necessary to obtain the correct gauge (see page 69).

Needle Suggestions: Size 3 for unpatterned area—16" and 29" circular; size 2 for patterned area—16" and 29" circular, and double pointed; size 1 for ribbing—29" circular, and double pointed.

Note: Follow graph making increases or decreases in rounds indicated. This is necessary in order to make the sts in the round evenly divisible by the number of sts in the pattern repeat.

YOKE: (All Sizes) With MC and rib needle, CO 121 sts. Work back and forth in k1, p1 rib for 1/2". With RS facing, rib 3 sts, work the One-Row Buttonhole (see page 74), rib to end. Work k1, p1 rib for 1/2", ending on RS row. With WS facing, work 8 rib sts and place on holder (left Button Band), purl 105 sts, at the same time inc 39 sts evenly, rib rem 8 sts. With RS facing, rib 8 sts and place on holder (right Buttonhole Band): 144 sts rem. Place marker (pm) at beg of rnd. (The marker will be at the center front of the garment.) Join, being careful not to twist sts. With MC, k2 rnds. Beg working from graph and change to 29" needles when necessary. When graph is complete, work in MC and inc 2 (6, 2) sts in first plain rnd: 378 (406, 434) sts in the yoke. **Mark the Body and Sleeves:** Starting at the beg of the rnd, pm after: 58 (63, 68) sts for right front, 73 (77, 81) sts for right sleeve, 116 (126, 136) sts for back, 73 (77, 81) sts for left sleeve, leaving 58 (63, 68) sts for left front (4 markers). **Short Rows:** Short rows are worked to provide a better fit. They are basically used to lower the front neck and are worked back and forth in St st. Starting at beg of rnd, work to last marker (left sleeve marker); slip marker. Work 5 sts of left front. *Yarn forward; slip next st p-wise to right-hand needle. Yarn back, turn work. Slip first st back to right-hand needle (wrapped st). WS facing, purl to last marker (right sleeve marker); slip marker. P5 sts of right front; slip next st p-wise to right-hand needle. Yarn back; turn work. Slip first st back to right-hand needle. Yarn back (wrapped st). Knit to wrapped st of left

front sts. Knit the wrap tog with the wrapped st, then k5 more sts of left front. Rep from*. Work 5 sts further into the front sts of the sweater on each side 4 times total (40 sts = 8 short rows). Beg working circularly again until yoke at center front meas 8 (9, 10)" or desired length from beg of colorwork.

DIVIDE SLEEVES AND BODY: Sleeves: With larger needles and Looping Provisional Cast On, CO 2 sets of 24 (28, 32) sts for the underarms and set aside. With larger 29" circular needle, knit across 58 (63, 68) sts of right front, drop yarn and needle. **Join new ball of yarn and larger 16" circular needle. Knit across 73 (77, 81) sts of right sleeve, then across cast-on sts placing marker after 12th (14th, 16th) st: 97 (105, 113) sts. Join and work even for a total of 20 rnds, ending at marker. Dec rnd: *K1, k2tog, work until 3 sts are left before marker, SSK, k1. Work 6 rnds even. Rep from* 16 (17, 18) more times: 63 (69, 75) sts. The sleeve is approximately 14 1/2 (15 1/4, 16)" long. Change to dpn when necessary. Work 6 rnds even after last dec rnd. Final dec rnd: *K1, k2tog; rep from*: 42 (46, 50) sts. Change to smaller dpn. Work k1, p1 rib for 2–3". BO in pattern. At right underarm, pick up larger 29" circular needle with yarn attached, remove the waste yarn from right underarm sts, knit up 24 (28, 32) sts; knit across 116 (126, 136) back sts, then drop yarn and needle. Rep from** for left sleeve. **Body:** At left underarm, pick up larger 29" circular needle with yarn attached, remove the waste yarn from left underarm sts, knit up 24 (28, 32) sts; knit across rem 58 (63, 68)

sts of left front: 280 (308, 336) sts. Continue working in the rnd until piece meas 14 (15, 16)" from underarm or desired length. BO 4 sts at center front. Baste down center front of sweater. Machine stitch twice on each side. Cut open.

BUTTONHOLE BAND: Beg at top of right front, using MC and rib needles, pick up the 8 sts of right Buttonhole Band from holder. *Work even in k1, p1 rib for approximately 3 (3 1/4, 3 1/2)" from last buttonhole. With WS facing, rib 3 sts, work the One-Row Buttonhole (see page 74), rib to end. Rep from * 6 more times. Continue in k1, p1 rib for 1 1/2 (1 3/4, 2)". Break yarn. Place sts on holder. The last buttonhole will be made in the bottom ribbing.

BUTTON BAND: Rep as for Buttonhole Band, omitting buttonholes, and do not break yarn.

BOTTOM RIBBING: With rib needle and RS facing, pick up sts from left Button Band (make sure band is not twisted), body sts from waste yarn, and right Button Band sts (make sure band is not twisted). With MC attached at left Button Band, work back and forth in k1, p1 rib for 1 1/2", end with RS. With WS facing, rib 3 sts, work the One-Row Buttonhole, rib to end. Work 1/2" of k1, p1 rib. BO in pattern.

FINISHING: Weave underarm seams. Sew button and Buttonhole Bands to center fronts. Sew in ends. Sew on buttons.

DEAN JACKET

Finished Size: 40 (44, 48)" approximate bust/chest width.

Materials: Kimmet Croft Fibers' Fairy Hare (60% Rambouillet wool, 40% Angora; 1 oz. = approx. 150 yards/137 meters): 8 (9, 10) oz. #FF1 (MC and BB); 1 oz. each #FF82, and #FF70; 2/3 oz. #FF78; 1/2 oz. each, #FF72, #FF66, #FF64, and #FF81. Jamieson & Smith's 2 Ply Jumper Weight (100% pure Shetland wool; 1 oz. = approx. 150 yards/137 meters): 2/3 oz. #203 Silver Gray.

Nine 7/16" buttons.

Gauge: 7 sts and 10 rows equal 1" over St st. Adjust needle sizes if necessary to obtain the correct gauge (see page 69).

Needle Suggestions: Size 3 for unpatterned areas; size 2 for patterned areas; size 1 for bands.

RIGHT FRONT: With smallest needle and BB (band color), CO 154 (161, 168) sts. K6 rows. K16 sts, *work One-Row Buttonhole (see page 74), k17 (18, 19) sts, rep from* 6 times total; work One-Row Buttonhole, k15 (16, 17) sts. K5 rows (total of 6 garter st ridges). Change to medium needles and work 2 rows St st in BB color. Beg working from graph. Work even for 1½ (2, 2½)". Keeping in pattern, inc 1 st at neck edge (right side) 4 times, inc 2 sts once, inc 3 sts once, inc 5 sts once, inc 7 sts once: 175 (182, 189) sts. When graph is complete, work in MC until piece meas approximately 5¾ (6¼, 6¾)" from beg. RS facing, BO 62 (69, 76) sts for armhole. Work to end, p 1 row. RS facing, BO 2 sts at armhole edge 4 times: 105 sts rem (all sizes). This is the side seam and should meas approximately 15". Work even for 1". Piece should meas approximately 10½

(11, 11½)" from beg. BO rem 105 sts. With smallest needles and BB, pick up and k80 (85, 90) sts along bottom edge. K7 more rows. Next row: K74 (79, 84) sts, work One-Row Buttonhole, knit to end of row. K6 more rows. Using medium needle, BO on reverse side of knit (8 garter ridges).

LEFT FRONT: CO and k12 rows omitting buttonholes. Work same as Right Front, reversing shaping.

BACK: With largest needle and MC, CO 142 (156, 170) sts. Change to smallest needle. Work 1" in garter st. Change to largest needle. Work even in St st until piece meas 16" from beg. BO 2 sts at the beg of next 8 rows. Work until piece meas 26 (27, 28)" from beg. Place rem sts on 3 holders: 40 (44, 48) sts for each shoulder, and 46 (52, 58) sts for back.

SLEEVES: With largest needle and MC, CO 62 (70, 80) sts. Change to smallest needle. Work 1" in garter st. Change to largest needle and St st. Inc 6 (10, 12) sts evenly across next row: 68 (80, 92) sts. Inc 1 st each side every 4th row 31 (31, 32) times and every 6th row 5 (6, 6) times: 140 (154, 168) sts. Work even until piece meas 17½ (18, 18½)" from beg. BO 2 sts beg of next 8 rows. Place rem sts on holder.

FINISHING: Join shoulder seams. With smallest needle and BB, pick up and k45 (48, 50) sts from right center front to shoulder seam, 46 (52, 58) sts from back neck holder, 45 (48, 50) sts from shoulder seam to left center front: 136 (148, 158) sts. K3 more rows (2 garter ridges). On the next row dec 13 (16, 18) evenly across row. K1 more row. On next row,

k3, work One-Row Buttonhole, knit to end of row. K1 more row. On next row dec 6 (9, 11) sts evenly across row: 117 (123, 129) sts. K3 more rows. Using medium needle, BO on reverse side in knit. BO or sew sleeves into armhole (see page 75). Sew side and sleeve seams.

DEAN CAP

Finished Sizes: 21 (23)" circumference.

Materials: Kimmet Croft Fibers' Fairy Hare (60% Rambouillet wool, 40% Angora; 1 oz. = approx. 150 yards/137 meters): 1/2 oz. #FF1 (MC); 1/4 oz. each #FF82, #FF70, #FF72, #FF66, #FF64, #FF81, and #FF78. Jamieson & Smith's 2 Ply Jumper Weight (100% pure Shetland wool; 1 oz. = approx. 150 yards/137 meters): 1/4 oz. #203 Silver Gray.

Gauge: 7 sts and 10 rows equal 1" over St st. Adjust needle sizes if necessary to obtain the correct gauge (see page 69).

Needle Suggestions: Size 2 for patterned area—16" circular, and double pointed; size 1 for ribbing—16" circular.

With MC and smaller needle, CO 136 (146) sts. Place marker at beg of rnd. Join, being careful not to twist sts. Work 3/4" in k1, p1 rib. Change to larger needle, work 1 rnd, inc 16 (22) sts evenly: 152 (168) sts. Work even following graph. After completing graph, work even in MC until piece meas approximately 7" from beg. With MC, work 1 rnd, dec 5 (7) sts evenly: 147 (161) sts. **Seven Point Crown:** Begin working with circular needle and change to dpn when necessary.

Work dbl dec at seven points as follows: sl 2 sts k-wise tog, k1, p2sso. *Rnd 1:* *K18 (20), dbl dec; rep from* 6 more times. *Rnd 2 and even numbered rnds:* Knit. *Rnd 3:* *K16 (18), dbl dec; rep from* 6 more times. Continue in this manner, working 1 less st before and after each dbl dec until 21 sts rem. Work dbl dec around: 7 sts rem. Draw yarn through 7 sts. Sew in ends.

THE BLUE SHIMMER

❧ *Designed by Anna-Lisa Mannheimer Lunn* ❧

THE BLUE SHIMMER YOKE PULLOVER

Finished Size: 40 (44, 48)" approximate bust/chest width.

Materials: Kimmet Croft Fibers' Fairy Hare (60% Rambouillet wool, 40% Angora; 1 oz. = approx. 150 yards/137 meters): 8 (9, 10) oz. #FF27 (MC); 1 oz. each #FF51, and #FF33; 1/4 oz. each #FF32, #FF19, #FF49 #FF55, and #FF59.

Gauge: 7 sts and 10 rows equal 1" over St st. Adjust needle sizes if necessary to obtain the correct gauge (see page 69).

Needle Suggestions: Size 3 for unpatterned area—16" and 29" circular, and double pointed; size 2 for patterned area—16" and 29" circular, and double pointed; size 1 for ribbing—29" circular, and double pointed.

Note: Follow graph making increases or decreases in rounds indicated. This is necessary to make the sts in the round evenly divisible by the number of sts in the pattern repeat.

YOKE: (All sizes) With MC, smaller 16" circular needle, and using the Looping Provisional Cast On (see page 70), CO 120 sts. Place marker (pm) at beg of rnd. (The marker will be at the back of the right shoulder on the garment.) Join, being careful not to twist sts. With MC, work 2" in k1, p1 rib. (Later, the ribbing will be folded in half to the inside of the neckline, the waste yarn removed, and the live sts stitched in place. This allows for plenty of give in the neck.) K1 rnd MC, inc 24 sts evenly: 144 sts. Beg working from graph and change to 29" needles when necessary. When graph is complete, work in MC and inc 0 (1, 2) sts in first plain rnd: 378 (406, 434) sts. Change to larger needles. **Mark the Body and Sleeves:** Starting at the beg of the rnd, pm after: 116 (126, 136) sts for back, 73 (77, 81) sts for left sleeve, 116 (126, 136) sts for front, and 73 (77, 81) sts for right sleeve (4 markers in place). Break yarn. **Short Rows:** Short rows are worked to provide a better fit. They are basically used to lower the front neck and are worked back and forth in St st. Starting at beg of rnd (back of the right shoulder), sl sts of right sleeve, right front marker and 6 sts of right front to left-hand side of needle. With RS facing, join new yarn. Keeping tail at back of work, bring yarn from back to front between needle tips, sl first st on left-hand side of needle to right-hand side, yarn back (wrapped st).

K5 sts of right front, sl marker, work to 5 sts beyond last marker (5 sts of left front worked). Continue with short rows: *Yarn forward; slip next st p-wise to right-hand needle. Yarn back; turn work. Slip first st back to right-hand needle (wrapped st). WS facing, purl to last marker (right front marker); slip marker, purl to the wrapped st, purl the wrap tog with the wrapped st on the needle, p5 more sts of right front; slip next st p-wise to right-hand needle. Yarn back; turn work. Slip first st back to right-hand needle. Yarn back (wrapped st). Knit to wrapped st of left front. Knit the wrap tog with the wrapped st on the needle, then k5 more sts of left front. Rep from*. Work 5 sts further into the front sts of the sweater on each side 4 times total (40 sts = 8 short rows) ending at left front. Beg working circularly again until yoke at center front meas 8 (9, 10)" (measured straight up) or desired length from the beg of the colorwork after the ribbing. End at back of the right shoulder marker.

DIVIDE SLEEVES AND BODY: Sleeves: With larger needles and Looping Provisional Cast On, CO 2 sets of 24 (28, 32) sts for the underarms and set aside. With larger 29" circular needle, knit across 116 (126, 136) back sts, drop yarn and needle. **Join new ball of yarn and larger 16" circular needle. Knit across 73 (77, 81) sts of left sleeve, then across cast-on sts placing marker after 12th (14th, 16th) st: 97 (105, 113) sts. Join and work even for a total of 20 rnds, ending at marker. Dec rnd: *K1, k2tog, work until 3 sts are left before marker, SSK, k1. Work 6 rnds even. Rep from* 16 (17, 18) more

"The Blue Shimmer" yoke cardigan.

times: 63 (69, 75) sts rem. The sleeve is approximately 14½ (15¼, 16)" long. Change to dpn when necessary. Work 6 rnds even after last dec rnd. Final dec rnd: *K1, k2tog; rep from*: 42 (46, 50) sts rem. Change to smaller dpn. Work k1, p1 rib for 2–3". BO in pattern. At left underarm, pick up larger 29" circular needle with yarn attached, remove the waste yarn from left underarm sts, knit up 24 (28, 32) sts; knit across 116 (126, 136) front sts, then drop yarn and needle. Rep from** for right sleeve. **Body:** At right underarm, pick up larger 29" circular needle with yarn attached, remove the waste yarn from right underarm sts, knit up 24 (28, 32) sts: 280 (308, 336) sts. Continue working in the rnd until desired length from neck rib less body rib length. Change to smaller dpn. Work in k1, p1 rib for 2–3". BO in pattern.

FINISHING: Weave underarm seams. Sew in ends. Fold neck ribbing in half to inside. Remove waste yarn and stitch in place.

THE BLUE SHIMMER
YOKE CARDIGAN

Finished Size: 40 (44, 48)" approximate bust/chest width.

Materials: Kimmet Croft Fibers' Fairy Hare (60% Rambouillet wool, 40% Angora; 1 oz. = approx. 150 yards/137 meters): 8 (9, 10) oz. #FF27 (MC); 1 oz. each #FF51, and #FF33; 1/3 oz. #FF32; 1/4 oz. each #FF19, #FF49 #FF55, and #FF59.
Nine 5/8" buttons.

Gauge: 7 sts and 10 rows equal 1" over St st. Adjust needle sizes if necessary to obtain the correct gauge (see page 69).

Needle Suggestions: Size 3 for unpatterned area—16" and 29" circular; size 2 for patterned area—16" and 29" circular, and double pointed; size 1 for ribbing—29" circular, and double pointed.

Note: Follow graph making increases or decreases in rounds indicated. This is necessary to make the sts in the round evenly divisible by the number of sts in the pattern repeat.

YOKE: (All Sizes) With MC and rib needle, CO 121 sts. Work back and forth in k1, p1 rib for 1/2". With RS facing, rib 3 sts, work the One-Row Buttonhole (see page 74), rib to end. Work k1, p1 rib for 1/2", ending on RS row. With WS facing, work 8 rib sts and place on holder (left Button Band), purl 105 sts, at the same time inc 39 sts evenly, rib rem 8 sts. With RS facing, rib 8 sts and place on holder (right Buttonhole Band): 144 sts rem. Place marker (pm) at beg of rnd. (The marker will be at the center front of the garment.) Join, being careful not to twist sts. With MC, k2 rnds. Beg working from graph and change to 29" needle when necessary. When graph is complete, work in MC and inc 0 (1, 2) sts in first plain rnd: 378 (406, 434) sts. **Mark the Body and Sleeves:** Starting at the beg of the rnd, pm after: 58 (63, 68) sts for right front, 73 (77, 81) sts for right sleeve, 116 (126, 136) sts for back, and 73 (77, 81) sts for left sleeve. Work rem 58 (63, 68) sts for left front (4 markers in place). **Short Rows:** Short rows are worked to

provide a better fit. They are basically used to lower the front neck and are worked back and forth in St st. Starting at beg of rnd, work to last marker (left sleeve marker); slip marker. Work 5 sts of left front. *Yarn forward; slip next st p-wise to right-hand needle. Yarn back, turn work. Slip first st back to right-hand needle (wrapped st). WS facing, purl to last marker (right sleeve marker); slip marker. P5 sts of right front; slip next st p-wise to right-hand needle. Yarn back; turn work. Slip first st back to right-hand needle. Yarn back (wrapped st). Knit to wrapped st of left front sts. Knit the wrap tog with the wrapped st, then k5 more sts of left front. Rep from*. Work 5 sts further into the front sts of the sweater on each side 4 times total (40 sts = 8 short rows). Beg working circularly again until yoke at center front meas 8 (9, 10)" or desired length from beg of colorwork.

DIVIDE SLEEVES AND BODY: Sleeves: With larger needles and Looping Provisional Cast On, CO 2 sets of 24 (28, 32) sts for the underarms and set aside. With larger 29" circular needle, knit across 58 (63, 68) sts of right front, drop yarn and needle. **Join new ball of yarn and larger 16" circular needle. Knit across 73 (77, 81) sts of right sleeve, then across cast-on sts placing marker after 12th (14th, 16th) st: 97 (105, 113) sts. Join and work even for a total of 20 rnds, ending at marker. Dec rnd: *K1, k2tog, work until 3 sts are left before marker, SSK, k1. Work 6 rnds even. Rep from* 16 (17, 18) more times: 63 (69, 75) sts. The sleeve is approximately 14½ (15¼, 16)" long. Change to dpn when necessary. Work 6

Legend:

- FF 19
- FF 27 (MC)
- FF 32
- FF 33
- FF 49
- FF 51
- FF 55
- FF 59
- purl on RS, knot on WS

CAP

Rnd 7: inc 2 sts: 164 sts.
Rnd 11: inc 4 sts: 168 sts.
Rnd 50: inc 2 sts: 170 sts.
Rnd 64: dec 8 sts: 162 sts.

PULLOVER AND CARDIGAN

Rnd 11: inc 73 sts: 217 sts.
Rnd 19: dec 1 st: 216 sts.
Rnd 34: inc 72 (84, 108) sts: 288 (300, 324) sts.
Rnd 37: inc 0 (4, 0) sts: 288 (304, 324) sts.
Rnd 43: dec 0 (4, 0) sts: 288 (300, 324) sts.
Rnd 50: inc 72 (100, 106) sts: 360 (400, 430) sts.
Rnd 64: inc 18 (5, 2) sts: 378 (405, 432) sts.

JACKET

Work even in pattern repeat as given.

rnds even after last dec rnd. Final dec rnd: *K1, k2tog; rep from*: 42 (46, 50) sts. Change to smaller dpn. Work k1, p1 rib for 2–3". BO in pattern. At right underarm, pick up larger 29" circular needle with yarn attached, remove the waste yarn from right underarm sts, knit up 24 (28, 32) sts; knit across 116 (126, 136) back sts, then drop yarn and needle. Rep from** for left sleeve. **Body:** At left underarm, pick up larger 29" circular needle with yarn attached, remove the waste yarn from left underarm sts, knit up 24 (28, 32) sts; knit across rem 58 (63, 68) sts of left front: 280 (308, 336) sts. Continue working in the rnd until piece meas 14 (15, 16)" from underarm or desired length. BO 4 sts at center front. Baste down center front of sweater. Machine stitch twice on each side. Cut open.

BUTTONHOLE BAND: Beg at top of right front, using MC and rib needles, pick up the 8 sts of right Buttonhole Band from holder. *Work even in k1, p1 rib for approximately 3 (3¼, 3½)" from last buttonhole. With WS facing, rib 3 sts, work the One-Row Buttonhole (see page 74), rib to end. Rep from * 6 more times. Continue in k1, p1 rib for 1½ (1¾, 2)". Break yarn. Place sts on holder. The last buttonhole will be made in the bottom ribbing.

BUTTON BAND: Rep as for Buttonhole Band, omitting buttonholes, and do not break yarn.

BOTTOM RIBBING: With rib needle and RS facing, pick up sts from left Button Band (make sure band is not twisted), body sts from waste yarn, and right Button Band sts (make sure band is not

twisted). With MC attached at left Button Band, work back and forth in k1, p1 rib for 1½", end with RS. With WS facing, rib 3 sts, work the One-Row Buttonhole, rib to end. Work 1/2" of k1, p1 rib. BO in pattern.

FINISHING: Weave underarm seams. Sew Button and Buttonhole Bands to center fronts. Sew in ends. Sew on buttons.

THE BLUE
SHIMMER JACKET

Finished Size: 40 (44, 48)" approximate bust/chest width.

Materials: Kimmet Croft Fibers' Fairy Hare (60% Rambouillet wool, 40% Angora; 1 oz. = approx. 150 yards/137 meters): 8 (9, 10) oz. #FF27 (MC and BB); 2 oz. each #FF51, and #FF33; 2/3 oz. #FF32; 1/2 oz. each #FF19, #FF49, #FF55, and #FF59.
Nine 7/16" buttons.

Gauge: 7 sts and 10 rows equal 1" over St st. Adjust needle sizes if necessary to obtain the correct gauge (see page 69).

Needle Suggestions: Size 3 for unpatterned area; size 2 for patterned area; size 1 for bands.

RIGHT FRONT: With smallest 24" needle and BB (band color), CO 154 (161, 168) sts. K6 rows. K16 sts, *work One-Row Buttonhole (see page 74), k17 (18, 19) sts, rep from* 6 times total; work One-Row Buttonhole, k15 (16, 17) sts. K5 rows (total of 6 garter st ridges). Change to medium needles and work 2 rows St st in BB color. Beg working from

graph. Work even for 1½ (2, 2½)". Keeping in pattern, inc 1 st at neck edge (right side) 4 times, inc 2 sts once, inc 3 sts once, inc 5 sts once, inc 7 sts once: 175 (182, 189) sts. When graph is complete, work in MC until piece meas approximately 5¾ (6¼, 6¾)" from beg. RS facing, BO 62 (69, 76) sts for armhole. Work 2 rows. RS facing, BO 2 sts at armhole edge 4 times: 105 sts rem (all sizes). This is the side seam and should meas approximately 15". Work even for 1". Piece should meas approximately 10½ (11, 11½)" from beg. BO rem 105 sts. With smallest needles and BB, pick up and k80 (85, 90) sts along bottom edge. K7 more rows. Next row: K74 (79, 84) sts, work One-Row Buttonhole, knit to end of row. K6 more rows. Using medium needle, BO on reverse side of knit (8 garter ridges).

LEFT FRONT: Work as for Right Front, omitting buttonholes and reversing shaping.

BACK: With largest needle and MC, CO 142 (156, 170) sts. Change to smallest needle. Work 1" in garter st. Change to largest needle. Work even in St st until piece meas 16" from beg. BO 2 sts at the beg of next 8 rows. Work until piece meas 26 (27, 28)" from beg. Place rem sts on 3 holders: 40 (44, 48) sts for each shoulder, and 46 (52, 58) sts for back.

SLEEVES: With largest needle and MC, CO 62 (70, 80) sts. Change to smallest needle. Work 1" in garter st. Change to largest needle and St st. Inc 6 (10, 12) sts evenly across next row: 68 (80, 92) sts. Inc 1 st each side every 4th row 31 (31, 32) times and every 6th row 5 (6, 6) times: 140 (154, 168) sts. Work even until piece meas 17½ (18, 18½)" from beg. BO 2 sts beg of next 8 rows. Place rem sts on holder.

FINISHING: Join shoulder seams. With smallest needle and BB, pick up and k45 (48, 50) sts from right center front to shoulder seam, 46 (52, 58) sts from back neck holder, 45 (48, 50) sts from shoulder seam to left center front: 136 (148, 158) sts. K3 more rows (2 garter ridges). On the next row dec 13 (16, 18) sts evenly across row. K1 more row. On next row, k3, work One-Row Buttonhole, knit to end of row. K1 more row. On next row dec 6 (9, 11) sts evenly across row: 117 (123, 129) sts. K3 more rows. Using medium needle, BO on reverse side in knit. BO or sew sleeves into armhole (see page 75). Sew side and sleeve seams.

Finished Size: 23" circumference.
Materials: Kimmet Croft Fibers' Fairy Hare (60% Rambouillet wool, 40% Angora; 1 oz. = approx. 150 yards/137 meters): 1/2 oz. #FF27 (MC), #FF51 and #FF33; 1/4 oz. #FF19, #FF32, #FF49, #FF55, and #FF59.
Gauge: 7 sts and 10 rows equal 1" over St st. Adjust needle sizes if necessary to obtain the correct gauge (see page 69).
Needle Suggestions: Size 2 for patterned area—16" circular, and double pointed; size 1 for ribbing—16" circular.

With MC and smaller needle, CO 146. Place marker at beg of rnd. Join, being careful not to twist sts. Work 3/4" in k1, p1 rib. Change to larger needle,

work 1 rnd, inc 16 sts evenly: 162 sts. Follow graph, working inc/dec marked on graph. After completing graph, work even in MC until piece meas approximately 7" from beg. With MC, work 1 rnd plain, dec 1 st evenly: 161 sts. **Seven Point Crown:** Begin working with circular needle and change to dpn when necessary. Work dbl dec at seven points as follows: sl 2 sts k-wise tog, k1, p2sso. *Rnd 1:* *K20, dbl dec; rep from* 6 more times. *Rnd 2 and all even numbered rnds:* Knit. *Rnd 3:* *K18, dbl dec; rep from* 6 more times. Continue in this manner, working 1 less st before and after each dbl dec until 21 sts rem. Work dbl dec around: 7 sts rem. Draw yarn through 7 sts. Sew in ends.

THE WILD APPLE

❧ Designed by Kerstin Olsson ❧

THE WILD APPLE YOKE PULLOVER

Finished Size: 40 (44, 48)" approximate bust/chest width.
Materials: Kimmet Croft Fibers' Fairy Hare (60% Rambouillet wool, 40% Angora; 1 oz. = approx. 150 yards/137 meters): 8 (9, 10) oz. #FF132 (MC); 1/2 oz. each #FF130, and #FF116; 1/3 oz. each #FF117, #FF124, #FF127, and #FF129; 1/4 oz. each #FF119, #FF122, #FF115, #FF114, #FF113, #FF112, #FF90, and #FF74.

Gauge: 7 sts and 10 rows equal 1" over St st. Adjust needle sizes if necessary to obtain the correct gauge (see page 69).
Needle Suggestions: Size 3 for unpatterned areas—16" and 29" circular, and double pointed; size 2 for patterned areas—16" and 29" circular, and double pointed; size 1 for ribbing—29" circular, and double pointed.

Note: Follow graph making increases or decreases in rounds indicated. This is necessary to make the sts in the round evenly divisible by the number of sts in the pattern repeat.

YOKE: (All sizes) With MC, smaller 16" needle, and using the Looping Provisional Cast On (see page 70), CO 120 sts. Place marker (pm) at beg of rnd. (The marker will be at the back of the right shoulder on the garment.) Join, being careful not to twist sts. With MC, work 2" in k1, p1 rib. (Later, the ribbing will be folded in half to the inside of the neckline, the waste yarn will be removed, and the live sts stitched in place.) K1 rnd, inc 24 sts evenly: 144 sts. Beg working from graph and change to 29" needles when necessary. When graph is complete, inc 1 (3, 5) sts in MC: 378 (406, 434) sts. **Mark the Body and Sleeves:** Starting at the beg of the rnd, pm after: 116 (126, 136) sts for back, 73 (77, 81) sts for left sleeve, 116 (126, 136) sts for front, and 73 (77, 81) sts for right sleeve (4 markers in place). Break yarn. **Short Rows:** Short rows are worked to provide a better fit. They are basically used to lower the front neck and are worked back and forth in St st. Starting at beg of round (back of the right shoul-

"The Wild Apple" yoke pullover.

der), sl sts of right sleeve, right front marker and 6 sts of right front to left-hand side of needle. Change to larger needles. With RS facing, join new yarn. Keeping tail at back of work, bring yarn from back to front between needle tips, sl first st on left-hand side of needle to right-hand side, yarn back (wrapped st). K5 sts of right front, sl marker, work to 5 sts beyond last marker (5 sts of left front worked). Continue with short rows: *Yarn forward; slip next st p-wise to right-hand needle. Yarn back; turn work. Slip first st back to right-hand needle (wrapped st). WS facing, purl to last marker (right front marker); slip marker, purl to the wrapped st, purl the wrap tog with the wrapped st on the needle, p5 more sts of right front; slip next st p-wise to right-hand needle. Yarn back; turn work. Slip first st back to right-hand needle. Yarn back (wrapped st). Knit to wrapped st of left front. Knit the wrap tog with the wrapped st on the needle, then k5 more sts of left front. Rep from*. Work 5 sts further into the front sts of the sweater on each side 4 times total (40 sts = 8 short rows) ending at left front. Beg working circularly again until yoke at center front meas 8 (9, 10)" (measured straight up) or desired length from the beg of the colorwork after the ribbing. End at back of the right shoulder marker.

DIVIDE SLEEVES AND BODY: Sleeves: With larger needles and Looping Provisional Cast On, CO 2 sets of 24 (28, 32) sts for the underarms and set aside. With larger 29" circular needle, knit across 116 (126, 136) back sts, drop yarn and needle. **Join new ball of yarn and

larger 16" circular needle. Knit across 73 (77, 81) sts of left sleeve, then across cast-on sts placing marker after 12th (14th, 16th) st: 97 (105, 113) sts. Join and work even for a total of 20 rnds, ending at marker. Dec rnd: *K1, k2tog, work until 3 sts are left before marker, SSK, k1. Work 6 rnds even. Rep from* 16 (17, 18) more times: 63 (69, 75) sts rem. The sleeve is approximately $14^{1}/_{2}$ ($15^{1}/_{4}$, 16)" long. Change to dpn when necessary. Work 6 rnds even after last dec rnd. Final dec rnd: *K1, k2tog; rep from*: 42 (46, 50) sts. Change to smaller dpn. Work k1, p1 rib for 2–3". BO in pattern. At left underarm, pick up larger 29" circular needle with yarn attached, remove the waste yarn from left underarm sts, knit up 24 (28, 32) sts; knit across 116 (126, 136) front sts, then drop yarn and needle. Rep from** for right sleeve. **Body:** At right underarm, pick up larger 29" circular needle with yarn attached, remove the waste yarn from right underarm sts, knit up 24 (28, 32) sts: 280 (308, 336) sts. Continue working in the round until desired length from neck rib less body rib length. Change to smaller dpn. Work k1, p1 rib for 2–3". BO in pattern.

FINISHING: Weave underarm seams. Sew in ends. Fold neck ribbing in half to inside. Remove waste yarn and st in place.

THE WILD APPLE
YOKE CARDIGAN

Finished Size: 40 (44, 48)" approximate bust/chest width.

Materials: Kimmet Croft Fibers' Fairy Hare (60% Rambouillet wool, 40% Angora; 1 oz. = approx. 150 yards/137 meters): 8 (9, 10) oz. #FF132 (MC); 1/2 oz. each #FF130, and #FF116; 1/3 oz. each #FF117, #FF124, #FF127, and #FF129; 1/4 oz. each #FF119, #FF122, #FF115, #FF114, #FF113, #FF112, #FF90, and #FF74.
Nine 5/8" buttons.

Gauge: 7 sts and 10 rows equal 1" over St st. Adjust needle sizes if necessary to obtain the correct gauge (see page 69).

Needle Suggestions: Size 3 for unpatterned area—16" and 29" circular; size 2 for patterned area—16" and 29" circular, and double pointed; size 1 for ribbings—29" circular, and double pointed.

Note: Follow graph making increases or decreases in rounds indicated. This is necessary to make the sts in the round evenly divisible by the number of sts in the pattern repeat.

YOKE: (All Sizes) With MC and rib needle, CO 121 sts. Work back and forth in k1, p1 rib for 1/2". With RS facing, rib 3 sts, work the One-Row Buttonhole (see page 74), rib to end. Work k1, p1 rib for 1/2", ending on RS row. With WS facing, work 8 rib sts and place on holder (left Button Band), purl 105 sts, at the same time inc 39 sts evenly, rib rem 8 sts. With RS facing, rib 8 sts and place on holder (right Buttonhole Band): 144 sts rem. Place marker (pm) at beg of rnd. (The marker will be at the center front of the garment.) Join, being careful not to twist sts. With MC, k2 rnds. Beg working from graph and change to 29" needle when

CAP
Beg on rnd 14, work to end.

JACKET
Work even in pattern as given.

PULLOVER OR CARDIGAN
Rnd 6: inc 76 sts: 220 sts.
Rnd 24: inc 79 (92, 105) sts: 299
(312, 325) sts.
Rnd 45: inc 78 (91, 104) sts: 377
(403, 429) sts.

Note: *This chart is not representative of true colors; the colors were chosen for clarity. Please refer to the photograph on page 100.*

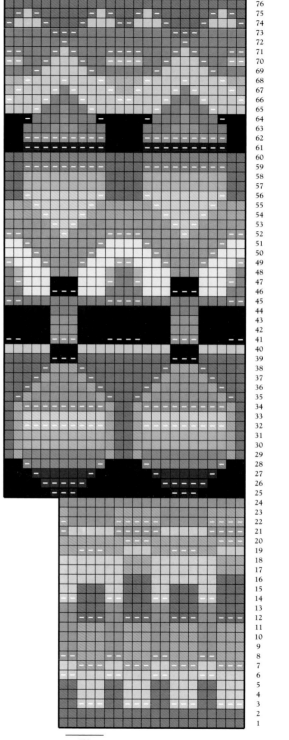

FF115
FF114
FF113
FF112
FF90
FF74
FF116
FF127
FF129
FF132
FF130
FF117
FF119
FF124
FF122
— purl on RS;
knit on WS.

necessary. When graph is complete, inc 1 (3, 5) sts in MC: 378 (406, 434) sts in the yoke. **Mark the Body and Sleeves:** Starting at the beg of the rnd, pm after: 58 (63, 68) sts for right front, 73 (77, 81) sts for right sleeve, 116 (126, 136) sts for back, and 73 (77, 81) sts for left sleeve. Work rem 58 (63, 68) sts for left front (4 markers in place). **Short Rows:** Short rows are worked to provide a better fit. They are basically used to lower the front neck and are worked back and forth in St st. Starting at beg of rnd, work to last marker (left sleeve marker); slip marker. Work 5 sts of left front. *Yarn forward; slip next st p-wise to right-hand needle. Yarn back, turn work. Slip first st back to right-hand needle (wrapped st). WS facing, purl to last marker (right sleeve marker); slip marker. P5 sts of right front; slip next st p-wise to right-hand needle. Yarn back; turn work. Slip first st back to right-hand needle. Yarn back (wrapped st). Knit to wrapped st of left front sts. Knit the wrap tog with the wrapped st, then k5 more sts of left front. Rep from*. Work 5 sts further into the front sts of the sweater on each side 4 times total (40 sts = 8 short rows). Beg working circularly again until yoke at center front meas 8 (9, 10)" or desired length from beg of colorwork.

DIVIDE SLEEVES AND BODY: Sleeves: With larger needles and Looping Provisional Cast On, CO 2 sets of 24 (28, 32) sts for the underarms and set aside. With larger 29" circular needle, knit across 58 (63, 68) sts of right front, drop yarn and needle. **Join new ball of yarn and larger 16" circular needle. Knit across

73 (77, 81) sts of right sleeve, then across cast-on sts placing marker after 12th (14th, 16th) st: 97 (105, 113) sts. Join and work even for a total of 20 rnds, ending at marker. Dec rnd: *K1, k2tog, work until 3 sts are left before marker, SSK, k1. Work 6 rnds even. Rep from* 16 (17, 18) more times: 63 (69, 75) sts. The sleeve is approximately 14½ (15¼, 16)" long. Change to dpn when necessary. Work 6 rnds even after last dec rnd. Final dec rnd: *K1, k2tog; rep from*: 42 (46, 50) sts. Change to smaller dpn. Work k1, p1 rib for 2–3". BO in pattern. At right underarm, pick up larger 29" circular needle with yarn attached, remove the waste yarn from right underarm sts, knit up 24 (28, 32) sts; knit across 116 (126, 136) back sts, then drop yarn and needle. Rep from** for left sleeve. **Body:** At left underarm, pick up larger 29" circular needle with yarn attached, remove the waste yarn from left underarm sts, knit up 24 (28, 32) sts; knit across rem 58 (63, 68) sts of left front: 280 (308, 336) sts. Continue working in the rnd until piece meas 14 (15, 16)" from underarm or desired length. BO 4 sts at center front. Baste down center front of sweater. Machine stitch twice on each side. Cut open.

BUTTONHOLE BAND: Beg at top of right front, using MC and rib needles, pick up the 8 sts of right Buttonhole Band from holder. *Work even in k1, p1 rib for approximately 3 (3¼, 3½)" from last buttonhole. With WS facing, rib 3 sts, work the One-Row Buttonhole (see page 74), rib to end. Rep from * 6 more times. Continue in k1, p1 rib for 1½ (1¾, 2)". Break yarn. Place sts on holder. The last but-

tonhole will be made in the bottom ribbing.

BUTTON BAND: Rep as for Buttonhole Band, omitting buttonholes, and do not break yarn.

BOTTOM RIBBING: With rib needle and RS facing, pick up sts from left Button Band (make sure band is not twisted), body sts from waste yarn, and right Button Band sts (make sure band is not twisted). With MC attached at left Button Band, work back and forth in k1, p1 rib for 1½", end with RS. With WS facing, rib 3 sts, work the One-Row Buttonhole, rib to end. Work ½" of k1, p1 rib. BO in pattern.

FINISHING: Weave underarm seams. Sew Button and Buttonhole Bands to center fronts. Sew in ends. Sew on buttons.

THE WILD APPLE JACKET

Finished Size: 40 (44, 48)" approximate bust/chest width.

Materials: Kimmet Croft Fibers' Fairy Hare (60% Rambouillet wool, 40% Angora; 1 oz. = approx. 150 yards/137 meters): 8 (9, 10) oz. #FF132 (MC and BB); 1 oz. each #FF130, and #FF116; 2/3 oz. each #FF117, #FF124, #FF127, and #FF129; ½ oz. each #FF119, #FF122, #FF115, #FF114, #FF113, #FF112, #FF90, #FF74.
Nine 7/16" buttons.

Gauge: 7 sts and 10 rows equal 1" over St st. Adjust needle sizes if necessary to obtain the correct gauge (see page 69).

Needle Suggestions: Size 3 for unpatterned area; size 2 for patterned area; size 1 for bands.

RIGHT FRONT: With smallest needle and BB (band color), CO 154 (161, 168) sts. K6 rows. K16 sts, *work One-Row Buttonhole (see page 70), k17 (18, 19) sts, rep from* 6 times total; work One-Row Buttonhole, k15 (16, 17) sts. K5 rows (total of 6 garter st ridges). Change to medium needles and work 2 rows St st in BB color. Beg working from graph. Work even for 1½ (2, 2½)". Keeping in pattern, inc 1 st at neck edge (right side) 4 times, inc 2 sts once, inc 3 sts once, inc 5 sts once, inc 7 sts once: 175 (182, 189) sts. When graph is complete, work in MC until piece meas approximately 5¾ (6¼, 6¾)" from beg. RS facing, BO 62 (69, 76) sts for armhole. Work 2 rows. RS facing, BO 2 sts at armhole edge 4 times: 105 sts rem (all sizes). This is the side seam and should meas approximately 15". Work even for 1". Piece should meas approximately 10½ (11, 11½)" from beg. BO rem 105 sts. With smallest needles and BB, pick up and k80 (85, 90) sts along bottom edge. K7 more rows. Next row: K74 (79, 84) sts, work One-Row Buttonhole, knit to end of row. K6 more rows. Using medium needle, BO on reverse side of knit (8 garter ridges).

LEFT FRONT: Work same as Right Front, omitting buttonholes and reversing shaping.

BACK: With largest needle and MC, CO 142 (156, 170) sts. Change to smallest needle. Work 1" in garter st. Change to largest needle. Work even in St st until piece meas 16" from beg. BO 2 sts at the beg of next 8 rows. Work until piece meas 26 (27, 28)" from beg. Place rem sts on 3 holders: 40 (44, 48) sts for each shoulder, and 46 (52, 58) sts for back.

SLEEVES: With largest needle and MC, CO 62 (70, 80) sts. Change to smallest needle. Work 1" in garter st. Change to largest needle and St st. Inc 6 (10, 12) sts evenly across next row: 68 (80, 92) sts. Inc 1 st each side every 4th row 31 (31, 32) times and every 6th row 5 (6, 6) times: 140 (154, 168) sts. Work even until piece meas 17½ (18, 18½)" from beg. BO 2 sts beg of next 8 rows. Place rem sts on holder.

FINISHING: Join shoulder seams. With smallest needle and BB, pick up and k45 (48, 50) sts from right center front to shoulder seam, 46 (52, 58) sts from back neck holder, 45 (48, 50) sts from shoulder seam to left center front: 136 (148, 158) sts. K3 more rows (2 garter ridges). On the next row dec 13 (16, 18) sts evenly across row. K1 more row. On next row, k3, work One-Row Buttonhole, knit to end of row. K1 more row. On next row dec 6 (9, 11) sts evenly across row: 117 (123, 129) sts. K3 more rows. Using medium needle, BO on reverse side in knit. BO or sew sleeves into armhole (see page 75). Sew side and sleeve seams.

THE WILD APPLE CAP

Finished Size: 21 (23)" circumference.
Materials: Kimmet Croft Fibers' Fairy Hare (60% Rambouillet wool, 40% Angora; 1 oz. = approx. 150 yards/137 meters): 1/2 oz. #FF132 (MC); 1/4 oz. each #FF130, #FF117, #FF119, #FF124, #FF122, #FF115, #FF114, #FF113, #FF112, #FF90, #FF74, #FF116, #FF127, and #FF129.

Gauge: 7 sts and 10 rows equal 1" over St st. Adjust needle sizes if necessary to obtain the correct gauge (see page 69).

Needle Suggestions: Size 2 patterned area—16" circular, and double pointed; size 1 ribbing—16" circular.

With MC and smaller needle, CO 136 (146) sts. Place marker at beg of rnd. Join, being careful not to twist sts. Work 3/4" in k1, p1 rib. Change to larger needle, work 1 rnd, inc 20 (23) sts evenly: 156 (169) sts. Follow graph, working inc/dec marked on graph. After completing graph, work even in MC until piece meas approximately 7" from beg. With MC, work 1 rnd, dec 9 (8) sts evenly: 147 (161) sts.

Seven Point Crown: Begin working with circular needle and change to dpn when necessary. Work dbl dec at seven points as follows: sl 2 sts k-wise tog, k1, p2sso. *Rnd 1:* *K18 (20), dbl dec; rep from* 6 more times. *Rnd 2 and even numbered rnds:* Knit. *Rnd 3:* *K16 (18), dbl dec; rep from* 6 more times. Continue in this manner, working 1 less st before and after each dbl dec until 21 sts rem. Work dbl dec around: 7 sts rem. Draw yarn through 7 sts. Sew in ends.

"The Green Meadow" mittens.

THE GREEN MEADOW

❧ *Designed by*
Anna-Lisa Mannheimer Lunn ❧

THE GREEN MEADOW
PULLOVER

Finished Size: 40 (42, 44, 46, 48)" approximate bust/chest width.

Materials: Alice Starmore's Scottish Campion (100% pure Shetland wool; 1 oz. = approx. 150 yards/137 meters): 10 (10, 11, 11, 12) skeins #93 Natural (MC); 1 skein each #85 Mogit, #127 Sage, #98 Ochre, and #18 Burnt Umber.

Gauge: 7 sts and 10 rows equal 1" over St st. Adjust needle sizes if necessary to obtain the correct gauge (see page 69).

Needle Suggestions: Size 3 for patterned area; size 2 for ribbing—straight and 16" circular.

BACK: With MC and smaller needles, CO 125 (133, 139, 147, 153) sts. Work k1, p1 rib for 3" ending on RS row. WS facing, purl across inc 14 sts evenly spaced: 139 (147, 153, 161, 167) sts. Change to larger needles and St st. Work even until piece meas 13½ (14, 14½, 15, 15½)" from beg. BO 2 sts at beg of next 8 rows: 123 (131, 137, 145, 151) sts rem. Work even until piece meas 23½ (24½, 25½, 26½, 27½)" from beg. Divide sts onto 3 holders: 36 (39, 42, 44, 46) sts for each shoulder, and 51 (53, 53, 57, 59) sts for back neck.

FRONT: With MC and smaller needles, CO 125 (133, 139, 147, 153) sts. Work k1, p1 rib for 3" ending on RS row. WS facing, purl across inc 14 sts evenly spaced: 139 (147, 153, 161, 167) sts. Change to larger needles. Follow graph instructions. Work even in established pattern until piece meas 13½ (14, 14½, 15, 15½)" from beg. BO 2 sts at beg of next 8 rows: 123 (131, 137, 145, 151) sts rem. Work even until piece meas 21 (22, 23, 24, 25)" from beg. **Shape neck:** Keeping in pattern, work 47 (50, 52, 55, 57) sts, place center 29 (31, 33, 35, 37) sts on holder. Attach new balls of yarn, work rem 47 (50, 52, 55, 57) sts. Keeping in pattern and working both sides at the same time, BO from each neck edge 4 sts once, 3 sts once, 2 sts once, then dec 1 st twice: 36 (39, 41, 44, 46) sts rem. Work even until piece meas 23½ (24½, 25½, 26½, 27½)" from beg. Place rem shoulder sts on holder.

SLEEVES: With smaller needles and MC, CO 63 (67, 71, 75, 79) sts. Work k1, p1 rib for 3" ending on RS row. WS facing, purl across inc 7 (9, 11, 13, 15) sts evenly spaced: 70 (76, 82, 88, 94) sts. Change to larger needles and St st. Inc 1 st each side every 4th row 30 (31, 31, 31, 31) times, then every 6th row 5 (5, 5, 6, 6) times: 140 (148, 154, 162, 168) sts. Work even until sleeve meas 17 (17½, 17½, 18, 18)" from beg. BO 2 sts at the beg of next 8 rows. Place rem 124 (132, 138, 146, 152) sts on holder.

FINISHING: BO fronts and back tog at shoulder seam (see page 75). Starting at the left shoulder seam, with MC and circular needle, pick up and knit 24 sts along left front neck edge, 29 (31, 33, 35, 37) sts from front holder, 24 sts along right neck edge, and 51 (53, 55, 57, 59) sts from back holder: 128 (132, 136, 140, 144) sts. Work k1, p1 rib for 1". BO in pattern. BO sleeves onto the body (see page 75). Sew side and sleeve seams.

THE GREEN MEADOW CARDIGAN

Finished Size: 40 (42, 44, 46, 48)" approximate bust/chest width.

Materials: Alice Starmore's Scottish Campion (100% pure Shetland wool; 1 oz. = approx. 150 yards/137 meters): 9 (9, 10, 10, 11) skeins #93 Natural (MC); 1 skein each #85 Mogit, #127 Sage, #98 Ochre, and #18 Burnt Umber.

Seven 7/16" buttons.

Gauge: 7 sts and 10 rows equal 1" over St st. Adjust needle sizes if necessary to obtain the correct gauge (see page 69).

Needle Suggestions: Size 3 for body and sleeves; size 2 for ribbing.

BACK: With MC and smaller needles, CO 133 (141, 147, 155, 161) sts. Work k1, p1 rib for 1". Change to larger needles and St st. Inc 1 st each side every 1", 4 times: 141 (149, 155, 163, 169) sts. Work even until piece meas 10½ (11, 11, 11½, 11½)" from beg. BO 2 sts at beg of next 8 rows: 125 (133, 139, 147, 153) sts rem. Work even until piece meas 20½ (21½, 22, 23, 23½)" from beg. Divide sts onto 3 holders: 38 (42, 44, 47, 49) sts for each shoulder, and 49 (49, 51, 53, 55) sts for back neck.

RIGHT FRONT: With MC and small-er needles, CO 75 (79, 81, 85, 89) sts. Work k1, p1 rib for 1/2". With RS facing, rib 2 sts, work the One-Row Buttonhole (see page 74), rib to end. Work even in rib for 1/2". With RS facing, rib 7 sts and place on holder (Buttonhole Band): 68 (72, 74, 78, 82) sts rem. Change to larg-er needles and St st. Follow graph in-structions and at the same time, inc 1 st at side seam every 1", 4 times: 72, (76, 78, 82, 86) sts. Work even until piece meas 10½ (11, 11, 11½, 11½)" from beg end-ing with a RS row. With WS facing, BO 2 sts at armhole edge 4 times: 64 (68, 70, 74, 78) sts rem. Work even until piece meas 18 (19, 19½, 20½, 21)" from beg ending with a WS row. **Shape neck:** At neck edge, keeping in pattern, BO 14 (14, 14, 15, 17) sts once, 4 sts once, 2 sts twice, then dec 1 st every other row 4 times: 38 (42, 44, 47, 49) sts rem. Keeping in pat-tern, work even until piece meas 20½ (21½, 22, 23, 23½)" from beg. Place rem shoulder sts on holder.

LEFT FRONT: Beg on WS row. Work as for Right Front reversing shaping and omitting buttonhole in bottom ribbing.

SLEEVES: With smaller needles and MC, CO 63 (67, 71, 75, 79) sts. Work k1, p1 rib for 1" ending on RS row. WS fac-ing, purl across inc 7 (9, 11, 13, 15) sts evenly: 70 (76, 82, 88, 94) sts. Change to larger needles and St st. Inc 1 st each side every 4th row 30 (31, 31, 31, 31) times, then every 6th row 5 (5, 5, 6, 6) times: 140 (148, 154, 162, 168) sts. Work even until sleeve meas 17 (17½, 17½, 18, 18)" from beg. BO 2 sts at the beg of next 8 rows. Place rem 124 (132, 138, 146, 152) sts on holder.

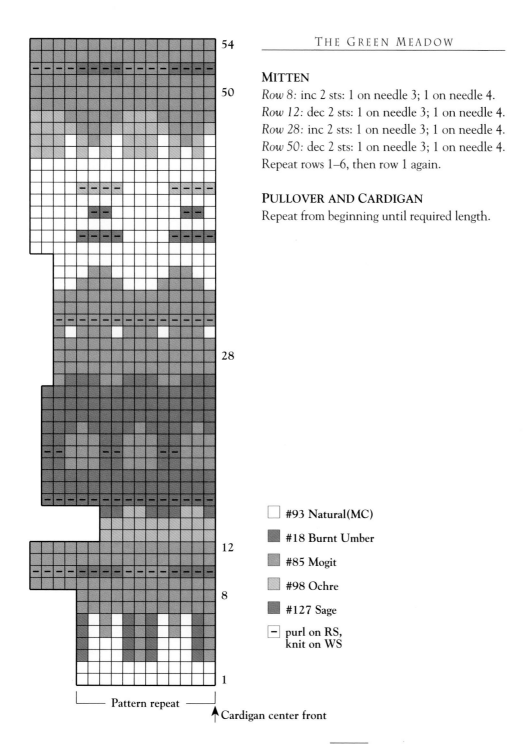

MITTEN

Row 8: inc 2 sts: 1 on needle 3; 1 on needle 4.

Row 12: dec 2 sts: 1 on needle 3; 1 on needle 4.

Row 28: inc 2 sts: 1 on needle 3; 1 on needle 4.

Row 50: dec 2 sts: 1 on needle 3; 1 on needle 4.

Repeat rows 1–6, then row 1 again.

PULLOVER AND CARDIGAN

Repeat from beginning until required length.

☐	#93 Natural(MC)
■	#18 Burnt Umber
▦	#85 Mogit
▨	#98 Ochre
▩	#127 Sage
−	purl on RS, knit on WS

Pattern repeat

↑ Cardigan center front

BUTTON BANDS: Right: With smaller needles and MC, pick up the 7 sts of right Buttonhole Band from holder. *Work even in k1, p1 rib for approximately 2¾ (3, 3, 3¼, 3⅓)" from last buttonhole. With RS facing, rib 2 sts, work the One-Row Buttonhole, rib to end. Rep from* 4 more times. Continue in k1, p1 rib for 2¼ (2½, 2½, 2¾, 2¾)". Do not break yarn. Place sts on holder. The last buttonhole will be made in the neckband. **Left:** Rep as for right Button Band, omitting buttonholes and breaking yarn.

FINISHING: BO fronts and back tog at shoulder seam (see page 75). With smaller needles, RS facing and MC attached, rib 7 sts of right Buttonhole Band from holder, pick up and knit 35 (35, 37, 37, 39) sts along right neck edge, 49 (49, 51, 53, 55) sts from back holder, 35 (35, 37, 37, 39) sts along left neck edge, rib 7 sts of left Button Band from holder: 133 (133, 139, 141, 147) sts. Work k1, p1 rib for 1/2", work the One-Row Buttonhole at neckline on right Buttonhole Band. Work an additional 1/2" of k1, p1 rib. BO in pattern. Sew Button Bands to center front edges. BO sleeves onto the body (see page 75). Sew side and sleeve seams. Sew on buttons.

(see page 75)

THE GREEN MEADOW MITTENS

Finished Size: Women's.
Materials: Alice Starmore's Scottish Campion (100% pure Shetland wool; 1 oz. = approx. 150 yards/137 meters): 1 oz. each #93 Natural (MC), #85 Mogit, #127 Sage, #98 Ochre, and #18 Burnt Umber.
Gauge: 7 sts and 10 rows equal 1" over St st. Adjust needle sizes if necessary to obtain the correct gauge (see page 69).
Needles Suggestions: Size 2 double pointed (set of five).
CUFF: (Select desired style.) **Reverse St st cuff:** With MC, CO 60 sts. Divide evenly between 4 needles (15 sts per needle). Join, being careful not to twist sts. Work even in St st for 2½". Turn cuff inside out, so the reverse St st becomes the right side. The needle where the yarn end is located is needle 1. The other needles are numbered clockwise from needle 1. With yarn in back, slip one st from needle 4 to needle 1, bring yarn forward, slip st back to needle 4. You have worked a turn st which will prevent a hole in the cuff. K1 rnd, dec 6 sts evenly: 60 sts. Work one rnd even. K1 rnd, inc 6 sts evenly. Continue at Mitten Body. **Rib cuff:** With MC, CO 54 sts. Divide between 4 needles (13, 14, 13, 14 sts per needle). Join, being careful not to twist sts. Work in k1, p1 rib for 3". Work one rnd in St st inc 6 sts evenly: 60 sts. Continue at Mitten Body. **Note:** 1. Needles 1 and 2 hold the palm sts for the mitten and are worked in MC. Needles 3 and 4 hold the patterned, back side of the mitten and are worked in multiple colors following graph. 2. Follow graph making increases or decreases in rnds indicated. This is necessary to make the sts in the rnd evenly divisible by the number of sts in the pattern repeat. 3. The cuff and mitten top are worked in the rnd in MC. The patterned portion of the mitten is worked back and forth in St st in multiple colors (see Mitten Body).

MITTEN BODY: Right Hand: Starting with needle 1, k1, p1, k3, place a marker, p1, k9. Knit across needle 2. Leave yarn at the end of needle 2. Go to needle 4 and attach a second ball of MC. Turn work. Purl across needles 4 and 3. Twist the yarn ends between needles 2 and 3 to close the side of the mitten. The patterned side of the mitten will be facing you. Work Row 1 of chart. Purl across needles 2 and 1. Twist the yarn ends between needles 1 and 4 to close the other side of the mitten. The palm of the mitten is always worked in MC. Continue working back and forth, twisting the yarn at row ends. At the same time, on the palm side work a thumb gusset by inc 1 st every knit row before the marker, 12 times. After the final thumb gusset inc row, twist yarns at end of row and purl back to marker. Place 17 sts after marker on a holder. CO 6 sts at end of purl row: 15 sts on needle 1. Work even in St st until graph is completed. **Shape Mitten Top:** With MC and starting at needle 1, k2 rnds. *K1, SSK, knit to last 3 sts on needle 2, k2tog, k1. Then, k1, SSK, knit to last 3 sts on needle 4, k2tog, K1. Rep from* until 8 sts rem. Draw yarn through sts and tighten to end off. **Thumb:** Put 17 sts on holder onto one dpn. Knit across 8 sts on needle 1, knit across next 8 sts for needle 2, knit rem st onto needle 3 and pick up and knit 7 sts along the CO sts. There will be a total of 24 sts, 8 per needle. Working in the rnd, work even in St st for 28 rnds. In the next rnd, k2tog across rnd: 12 sts rem. In the next rnd, k2tog across rnd: 6 sts rem. Draw yarn through sts and tighten to end off. **Left Hand:** After the cuff is worked, knit across needle 1, k9 sts on needle 2, p1, place marker, k3, p1, k1. Continue to work the same as Right Hand.

FINISHING: Sew in ends. For the reverse St st cuff, if desired, brush cuff with a stiff brush (such as a vegetable brush) to raise the nap.

THE LARGE CARNATION

❧ *Designed by Emma Jacobsson* ❧

THE LARGE CARNATION PULLOVER

Finished Size: 40 (42, 44, 46, 48)" approximate bust/chest width.

Materials: Jamieson & Smith's 2 Ply Jumper Weight (100% pure Shetland wool; 1 oz. = approx. 150 yards/137 meters): 10 (11, 11, 11, 12) skeins #202 Beige (MC); 3 (4, 4, 4, 4) skeins #4 Moorit (CC).

Gauge: 7 sts and 10 rows equal 1" over St st. Adjust needle sizes if necessary to obtain the correct gauge (see page 69).

Needle Suggestions: Size 3 for body and sleeves; size 2 for ribbing—straight and 16" circular.

BACK: With MC and smaller needles, CO 125 (133, 139, 147, 153) sts. Work k1, p1 rib for 3" ending on RS row. WS facing, purl across inc 14 sts evenly spaced: 139 (147, 153, 161, 167) sts. Change to larger needles and St st. Work even in St st until piece meas 13½ (14, 14½, 15, 15½)" from beg. BO 2 sts at beg of next 8 rows: 123 (131, 137, 145, 151) sts rem. Work even until piece meas 23½ (24½, 25½, 26½, 27½)" from beg. Divide sts onto 3 holders: 36 (39, 41, 44, 46) sts for each shoulder, and 51 (53, 55, 57, 59) sts for back neck.

FRONT: With MC and smaller needles, CO 125 (133, 139, 147, 153) sts. Work k1, p1 rib for 3" ending on RS row. WS facing, purl across inc 14 sts evenly spaced: 139 (147, 153, 161, 167) sts. Change to larger needles. Follow graph instructions. Work even in established pattern until piece meas 13½ (14, 14½, 15, 15½)" from beg. BO 2 sts at beg of next 8 rows: 123 (131, 137, 145, 151) sts rem. Work even until piece meas 21 (22, 23, 24, 25)" from beg. **Shape neck:** Keeping in pattern, work 47 (50, 52, 55, 57) sts, place center 29 (31, 33, 35, 37) sts on holder. Attach new balls of yarn, work rem 47 (50, 52, 55, 57) sts. Keeping in pattern and working both sides at the same time, BO from each neck edge 4 sts once, 3 sts once, 2 sts once, then dec 1 st twice: 36 (39, 41, 44, 46) sts rem. Keep-

ing in pattern, work even until piece meas 23½ (24½, 25½, 26½, 27½)" from beg. Place rem shoulder sts on holder.

SLEEVES: With smaller needles and MC, CO 63 (67, 71, 75, 79) sts. Work k1, p1 rib for 3" ending on RS row. WS facing, purl across inc 7 (9, 11, 13, 15) sts evenly spaced: 70 (76, 82, 88, 94) sts. Change to larger needles and St st. Inc 1 st each side every 4th row 30 (31, 31, 31, 31) times, then every 6th row 5 (5, 5, 6, 6) times: 140 (148, 154, 162, 168) sts. Work even until sleeve meas 17 (17½, 17½, 18, 18)" from beg. BO 2 sts at the beg of next 8 rows. Place rem 124 (132, 138, 146, 152) sts on holder.

FINISHING: BO fronts and back tog at shoulder seam (see page 75). Starting at the left shoulder seam, with MC and circular needle, pick up and knit 24 sts along left front neck edge, 29 (31, 33, 35, 37) sts from front holder, 24 sts along right neck edge, and 51 (53, 55, 57, 59) sts from back holder: 128 (132, 136, 140, 144) sts. Work k1, p1 rib for 1". BO in pattern. BO sleeves onto the body (see page 75). Sew side and sleeve seams.

THE LARGE CARNATION CARDIGAN

Finished Size: 40 (42, 44, 46, 48)" approximate bust/chest width.

Materials: Jamieson & Smith's 2 Ply Jumper Weight (100% pure Shetland wool; 1 oz. = approx. 150 yards/137 meters): 10 (10, 11, 11, 11) skeins #202 Beige (MC); 3 (3, 4, 4, 4) skeins

#4 Moorit (CC).

Seven 7/16" buttons.

Gauge: 7 sts and 10 rows equal 1" over St st. Adjust needle sizes if necessary to obtain the correct gauge (see page 69).

Needle Suggestions: Size 3 for body and sleeves; size 2 for ribbing—flat and 16" circular.

BACK: With MC and smaller needles, CO 133 (141, 147, 155, 161) sts. Work k1, p1 rib for 1". Change to larger needles and St st. Inc 1 st each side every 1", 4 times: 141 (149, 155, 163, 169) sts. Work even until piece meas 10½ (11, 11, 11½, 11½)" from beg. BO 2 sts at beg of next 8 rows: 125 (133, 139, 147, 153) sts rem. Work even until piece meas 20½ (21½, 22, 23, 23½)" from beg. Divide sts onto 3 holders: 38 (42, 44, 47, 49) sts for each shoulder, and 49 (49, 51, 53, 55) sts for back neck.

RIGHT FRONT: With MC and smaller needles, CO 75 (79, 81, 85, 89) sts. Work k1, p1 rib for 1/2". With RS facing, rib 2 sts, work the One-Row Buttonhole (see page 74), rib to end. Work even in rib for 1/2". With RS facing, rib 7 sts and place on holder (Buttonhole Band): 68 (72, 74, 78, 82) sts rem. Change to larger needles and St st. Follow graph instructions and at the same time inc 1 st

at side seam every 1", 4 times: 72, (76, 78, 82, 86) sts. Work even until piece meas 10½ (11, 11, 11½, 11½)" from beg ending with a RS row. With WS facing, BO 2 sts at armhole edge 4 times: 64 (68, 70, 74, 78) sts rem. Work even until piece meas 18 (19, 19½, 20½, 21)" from beg ending with a WS row. **Shape neck:** At neck edge, keeping in pattern, BO 14 (14, 14, 15, 17) sts once, 4 sts once, 2 sts twice, then dec 1 st every other row 4 times: 38 (42, 44, 47, 49) sts rem. Keeping in pattern, work even until piece meas 20½ (21½, 22, 23, 23½)" from beg. Place rem shoulder sts on holder.

LEFT FRONT: Work as for Right Front reversing shaping and omitting buttonhole in bottom ribbing.

SLEEVES: With smaller needles and MC, CO 63 (67, 71, 75, 79) sts. Work k1, p1 rib for 1" ending on RS row. WS facing, purl across inc 7 (9, 11, 13, 15) sts evenly: 70 (76, 82, 88, 94) sts. Change to larger needles and St st. Inc 1 st each side every 4th row 30 (31, 31, 31, 31) times, then every 6th row 5 (5, 5, 6, 6) times: 140 (148, 154, 162, 168) sts. Work even until sleeve meas 17 (17½, 17½, 18, 18)" from beg. BO 2 sts at the beg of next 8 rows. Place rem 124 (132, 138, 146, 152) sts on holder.

BUTTON BANDS: Right: With smaller needles and MC, pick up the 7 sts of right Buttonhole Band from holder. *Work even in k1, p1 rib for approximately 2¾ (3, 3, 3¼, 3⅓)" from last buttonhole. With the right side facing, rib 2 sts, work the One-Row Buttonhole, rib to end. Rep from* 4 more times. Continue in k1, p1 rib for 2¼ (2½, 2½, 2¾, 2¾)". Do not break yarn. Place sts on holder. The last buttonhole will be made in the neckband. **Left:** Rep as for right Button Band, omitting buttonholes and breaking yarn.

FINISHING: BO fronts and back tog at shoulder seam (see page 75). With smaller needles, RS facing, and MC attached, rib 7 sts of right Buttonhole Band from holder, pick up and knit 35 (35, 37, 37, 39) sts along right neck edge, 49 (49, 51, 53, 55) sts from back holder, 35 (35, 37, 37, 39) sts along left neck edge, rib 7 sts of left Button Band from holder : 133 (133, 139, 141, 147) sts. Work k1, p1 rib for 1/2", work the One-Row Buttonhole at neckline on right Buttonhole Band. Work an additional 1/2" of k1, p1 rib. BO in pattern. Sew Button Bands to center front edges. BO sleeves onto the body (see page 75). Sew side and sleeve seams. Sew on buttons.

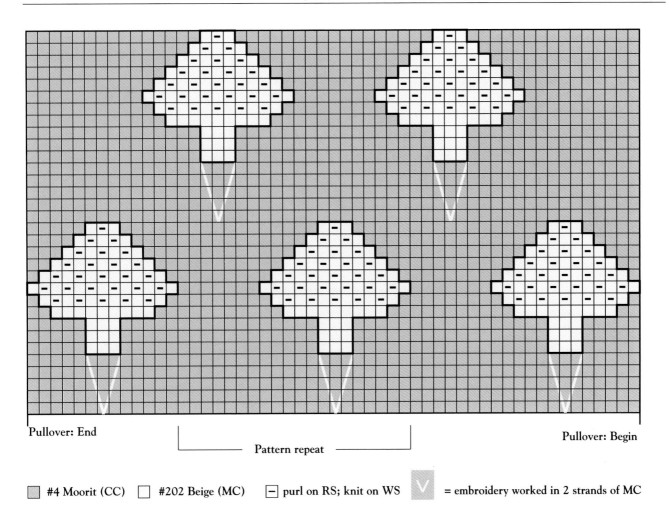

Pullover: End

Pattern repeat

Pullover: Begin

◼ #4 Moorit (CC) ☐ #202 Beige (MC) ⊟ purl on RS; knit on WS ⍦ = embroidery worked in 2 strands of MC

CARDIGAN

Right Front: Beginning at center front, with CC k4 sts, work entire graph once, K4 sts with CC, change to MC and k7 (11, 13, 17, 21) sts.

Left Front: Beginning at side edge with MC, k7 (11, 13, 17, 21) sts, with CC k4 sts, work entire graph once, end k4 sts with CC.

PULLOVER

With MC, k28 (32, 35, 39, 42) sts with CC k5 sts. Beg graph as indicated, work pattern repeat 2 times, k5 sts with CC, and k28 (32, 35, 39, 42) sts with MC.

THE FINNISH SPIKE

❧ Designed by Emma Jacobsson ❧

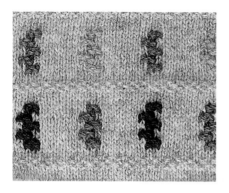

THE FINNISH SPIKE
PULLOVER

Finished Size: 40 (42, 44, 46, 48)" approximate bust/chest width.

Materials: Alice Starmore's Scottish Campion (100% pure Shetland wool; 1 oz. = approx. 150 yards/137 meters): 11 (11, 12, 12, 12) skeins #93 Natural (MC); 1 skein each #18 Burnt Umber, #98 Ochre, and #127 Sage.

Gauge: 7 sts and 10 rows equal 1" over St st. Adjust needle sizes if necessary to obtain the correct gauge (see page 69).

Needle Suggestions: Size 3 for body and sleeves; size 2 for ribbing—16" circular.

BACK: With MC and smaller needles, CO 125 (133, 139, 147, 153) sts. Work k1, p1 rib for 3" ending on RS row. WS facing, purl across inc 14 sts evenly spaced: 139 (147, 153, 161, 167) sts. Change to larger needles and St st. Work even in St st until piece meas 13½ (14, 14½, 15, 15½)" from beg. BO 2 sts at beg of next 8 rows: 123 (131, 137, 145, 151) sts rem. Work even until piece meas 23½ (24½, 25½, 26½, 27½)" from beg. Divide sts onto 3 holders: 36 (39, 41, 44, 46) sts for each shoulder, and 51 (53, 55, 57, 59) sts for back neck.

FRONT: With MC and smaller needles, CO 125 (133, 139, 147, 153) sts. Work k1, p1 rib for 3" ending on RS row. WS facing, purl across inc 13 sts evenly spaced: 138 (146, 152, 160, 166) sts. Change to larger needles. With MC, k9 (3, 6, 10, 3) sts, follow graph instructions, k9 (3, 6, 10, 3) rem sts in MC. Work even in established pattern until piece meas 13½ (14, 14½, 15, 15½)" from beg. BO 2 sts at beg of next 8 rows: 122 (130, 136, 144, 150) sts rem. Work even until piece meas 21 (22, 23, 24, 25)" from beg. **Shape neck:** Keeping in pattern, work 47 (50, 52, 55, 57) sts, place center 28 (30, 32, 34, 36) sts on holder. Attach new balls of yarn, work rem 47 (50, 52, 55, 57) sts. Keeping in pattern and working both sides at the same time, BO from each neck edge 4 sts once, 3 sts once, 2 sts once, then dec 1 st twice: 36 (39, 41, 44, 46) sts rem. Keeping in pattern, work even until piece meas 23½ (24½, 25½, 26½, 27½)" from beg. Place rem shoulder sts on holder.

SLEEVES: With smaller needles and MC, CO 63 (67, 71, 75, 79) sts. Work k1, p1 rib for 3" ending on RS row. WS facing, purl across inc 7 (9, 11, 13, 15) sts evenly spaced: 70 (76, 82, 88, 94) sts. Change to larger needles and St st. Inc 1 st each side every 4th row 30 (31, 31, 31, 31) times, then every 6th row 5 (5, 5, 6, 6) times: 140 (148, 154, 162, 168) sts. Work even until sleeve meas 17 (17½, 17½, 18, 18)" from beg. BO 2 sts at the beg of next 8 rows. Place rem 124 (132, 138, 146, 152) sts on holder.

FINISHING: BO fronts and back tog at shoulder seam (see page 75). Starting at the left shoulder seam, with MC and circular needle, pick up and knit 25 sts along left front neck edge, 28 (30, 32, 34, 36) sts from front holder, 24 sts along right neck edge, and 51 (53, 55, 57, 59) sts from back holder: 128 (132, 136, 140, 144) sts. Work k1, p1 rib for 1". BO in pattern. BO sleeves onto the body (see page 75). Sew side and sleeve seams.

THE FINNISH SPIKE
CARDIGAN

Finished Size: 40 (42, 44, 46, 48)" approximate bust/chest width.

Materials: Alice Starmore's Scottish Campion (100% pure Shetland wool; 1 oz. = approx. 150 yards/137 meters): 11 (12, 12, 12, 13) skeins #93 Natural (MC); 1 skein each #18 Burnt Umber, #98 Ochre, and #127 Sage. Seven 7/16" buttons.

Gauge: 7 sts and 10 rows equal 1" over St st. Adjust needle sizes if necessary to obtain the correct gauge (see page 69).

Needle Suggestions: Size 3 for body and sleeves; size 2 for ribbing.

BACK: With MC and smaller needles, CO 133 (141, 147, 155, 161) sts. Work k1, p1 rib for 1". Change to larger needles and St st. Inc 1 st each side every 1",

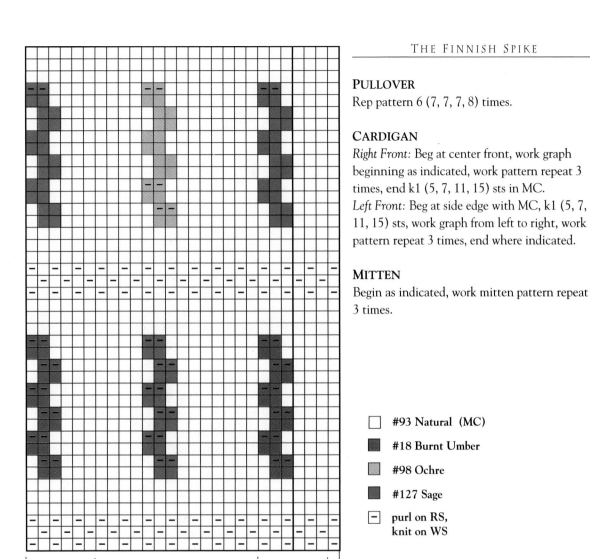

Pattern repeat

Mitten pattern repeat

PULLOVER
Rep pattern 6 (7, 7, 7, 8) times.

CARDIGAN
Right Front: Beg at center front, work graph beginning as indicated, work pattern repeat 3 times, end k1 (5, 7, 11, 15) sts in MC.
Left Front: Beg at side edge with MC, k1 (5, 7, 11, 15) sts, work graph from left to right, work pattern repeat 3 times, end where indicated.

MITTEN
Begin as indicated, work mitten pattern repeat 3 times.

☐	#93 Natural (MC)
■	#18 Burnt Umber
▨	#98 Ochre
■	#127 Sage
–	purl on RS, knit on WS

Begin cardigan Right Front
End cardigan Left Front

4 times: 141 (149, 155, 163, 169) sts. Work even until piece meas 10½ (11, 11, 11½, 11½)" from beg. BO 2 sts at beg of next 8 rows: 125 (133, 139, 147, 153) sts rem. Work even until piece meas 20½ (21½, 22, 23, 23½)" from beg. Divide sts onto 3 holders: 38 (42, 44, 47, 49) sts for each shoulder, and 49 (49, 51, 53, 55) sts for back neck.

RIGHT FRONT: With MC and smaller needles, CO 75 (79, 81, 85, 89) sts. Work k1, p1 rib for 1/2". With RS facing, rib 2 sts, work the One-Row Buttonhole (see page 74), rib to end. Work even in rib for 1/2". With RS facing, rib 7 sts and place on holder (Buttonhole Band): 68 (72, 74, 78, 82) sts rem. Change to larger needles and St st. Follow graph instructions and at the same time inc 1 st at side seam every 1", 4 times: 72, (76, 78, 82, 86) sts. Work even until piece meas 10½ (11, 11, 11½, 11½)" from beg ending with a RS row. With WS facing, BO 2 sts at armhole edge 4 times: 64 (68, 70, 74, 78) sts rem. Work even until piece meas 18 (19, 19½, 20½, 21)" from beg ending with a WS row. **Shape neck:** At neck edge, keeping in pattern, BO 14 (14, 14, 15, 17) sts once, 4 sts once, 2 sts twice, then dec 1 st every other row 4 times: 38 (42, 44, 47, 49) sts rem. Keeping in pattern, work even until piece meas 20½ (21½, 22, 23, 23½)" from beg. Place rem shoulder sts on holder.

LEFT FRONT: Work as for Right Front reversing shaping and omitting buttonhole in bottom ribbing.

SLEEVES: With smaller needles and MC, CO 63 (67, 71, 75, 79) sts. Work k1, p1 rib for 1" ending on RS row. WS facing, purl across inc 7 (9, 11, 13, 15) sts evenly: 70 (76, 82, 88, 94) sts. Change to larger needles and St st. Inc 1 st each side every 4th row 30 (31, 31, 31, 31) times, then every 6th row 5 (5, 5, 6, 6) times: 140 (148, 154, 162, 168) sts. Work even until sleeve meas 17 (17½, 17½, 18, 18)" from beg. BO 2 sts at the beg of next 8 rows. Place rem 124 (132, 138, 146, 152) sts on holder.

BUTTON BANDS: Right: With smaller needles and MC, pick up the 7 sts of right Buttonhole Band from holder. *Work even in k1, p1 rib for approximately 2¾ (3, 3, 3¼, 3⅓)" from last buttonhole. With RS facing, rib 2 sts, work the One-Row Buttonhole, rib to end. Rep from* 4 more times. Continue in k1, p1 rib for 2¼ (2½, 2½, 2¾, 2¾)". Do not break yarn. Place sts on holder. The last buttonhole will be made in the neckband. **Left:** Rep as for right Button Band, omitting buttonholes and breaking yarn.

FINISHING: BO fronts and back tog at shoulder seam (see page 75). With smaller needles, RS facing, and MC attached, rib 7 sts of right Buttonhole Band from holder, pick up and knit 35 (35, 37, 37, 39) sts along right neck edge, 49 (49, 51, 53, 55) sts from back holder, 35 (35, 37, 37, 39) sts along left neck edge, rib 7 sts of left Button Band from holder: 133 (133, 139, 141, 147) sts. Work k1, p1 rib for 1/2", work the One-Row Buttonhole at neckline on right front band. Work an additional 1/2" of k1, p1 rib. BO in pattern. Sew Button Bands to center front edges. BO sleeves onto the body (see page 75). Sew side and sleeve seams. Sew on buttons.

Finished Size: Women's.
Materials: Alice Starmore's Scottish Campion (100% pure Shetland wool; 1 oz. = approx. 150 yards/137 meters): 1 oz. #93 Natural (MC), 1/4 oz. each #18 Burnt Umber, #98 Ochre, and #127 Sage.
Gauge: 7 sts and 10 rows equal 1" over St st. Adjust needle sizes if necessary to obtain the correct gauge (see page 69).
Needle Suggestions: Size 2 double pointed (set of five).

CUFF: (Select desired style.) **Reverse St st cuff:** With MC, CO 60 sts. Divide evenly between 4 needles (15 sts per needle). Join, being careful not to twist sts. Work even in St st for 2½". Turn cuff inside out, so the reverse St st becomes the right side. The needle where the yarn end is located is needle 1. The other needles are numbered clockwise from needle 1. With yarn in back, slip one st from needle 4 to needle 1, bring yarn forward, slip st back to needle 4. You have worked a turn st which will prevent a hole in the cuff. Work one rnd in St st, dec 6 sts evenly at the same time. Work one rnd even. Work one more rnd, inc 6 sts evenly: 60 sts. Continue at Mitten Body. **Rib cuff:** With MC, CO 54 sts. Divide between 4 needles (13, 14, 13, 14 sts per needle). Join, being careful not to twist sts. Work in k1, p1 rib for 3". Work one rnd in St st inc 6 sts evenly: 60 sts. Continue at Mitten Body. **Note:** 1. Needles 1 and 2 hold the palm sts for the mitten and are worked in MC. Needles 3 and 4 hold the patterned, back side of the mitten and are worked in multiple colors following graph. 2. Follow graph making increases or decreases in rounds indicated. This is necessary to make the sts in the round evenly divisible by the number of sts in the pattern repeat. 3. The cuff and mitten top are worked in the round in MC. The patterned portion of the mitten is worked back and forth in St st in multiple colors (see Mitten Body).

MITTEN BODY: Right Hand: Starting with needle 1, k1, p1, k3, place marker, p1, k9. Knit across needle 2. Leave yarn at the end of needle 2. Go to needle 4 and attach a second ball of MC. Turn work. Purl across needles 4 and 3. Twist the yarn ends between needles 2 and 3 to close the side of the mitten. The patterned side of the mitten will be facing you. Work Row 1 of chart. Purl across needles 2 and 1. Twist the yarn ends between needles 1 and 4 to close the other side of the mitten. The palm of the mitten is always worked in MC. Continue working back and forth, twisting the yarn at row ends. At the same time, on the palm side work a thumb gusset by inc 1 st every knit row before the marker, 12 times. After the final thumb gusset inc row, twist yarns at end of row and purl back to marker. Place 17 sts after marker on a holder. CO 6 sts at end of purl row: 15 sts on needle 1. Work even in St st until graph is completed. **Shape Mitten Top:** With MC and starting at needle 1, k2 rnds. *K1, SSK, knit to last 3 sts on needle 2, k2tog, k1. Then, k1, SSK, knit to last 3 sts on needle 4, K2tog, K1. Rep

from* until 8 sts rem. Draw yarn through sts and tighten to end off. **Thumb:** Put 17 sts on holder onto one dpn. Knit across 8 sts on needle 1, knit across next 8 sts for needle 2, knit rem st onto needle 3 and pick up and knit 7 sts along the CO sts. There will be a total of 24 sts, 8 per needle. Working in the rnd, work even in St st for 28 rnds. In the next rnd, k2tog across rnd: 12 sts rem. In the next rnd, k2tog across rnd: 6 sts rem. Draw yarn through sts and tighten to end off. **Left Hand:** After the cuff is worked, knit across needle 1, k9 sts on needle 2, p1, place marker, k3, p1, k1. Continue to work the same as Right Hand.

FINISHING: Sew in ends. For the reverse St st cuff, if desired, brush cuff with a stiff brush (such as a vegetable brush) to raise the nap.

THE LARGE COLLAR

❧ Designed by Karin Ivarsson ❧

THE LARGE COLLAR
YOKE CARDIGAN

Finished Size: 40 (44, 48)" approximate bust/chest width.

Materials: Kimmet Croft Fibers' Fairy Hare (60% Rambouillet wool, 40% Angora; 1 oz. = approx. 150 yards/137 meters): 8 (9, 10) oz. #FF46 (MC); 1 oz. Ang 5; 1/2 oz. #FF24, #FF15, and #FF41; 1/4 oz. each #FF23, #FF19,

#FF40, #FF11, and #FF44. Alice Starmore's Scottish Campion (100% pure Shetland wool; 1 oz. = approx. 150 yards/137 meters): 1/4 oz. #85 Mogit Nine 5/8" buttons.

Gauge: 7 sts and 10 rows equal 1" over St st. Adjust needle sizes if necessary to obtain the correct gauge (see page 69).

Needle Suggestions: Size 3 for unpatterned areas—16" and 29" circular; size 2 for patterned areas—16" and 29" circular, and double pointed; size 1 for ribbing—29" circular, and double pointed.

Note: Follow graph making increases or decreases in rounds indicated. This is necessary to make the sts in the round evenly divisible by the number of sts in the pattern repeat.

YOKE: (All Sizes) With CC and rib needle, CO 121 sts. Work back and forth in k1, p1 rib for 1/2". With RS facing, rib 3 sts, work the One-Row Buttonhole (see page 74), rib to end. Work k1, p1 rib for 1/2", ending on RS row. With WS facing, work 8 rib sts and place on holder (left Button Band), purl 105 sts, at the same time inc 39 sts evenly, rib rem 8 sts. With RS facing, rib 8 sts and place on holder (right Buttonhole Band): 144 sts rem. Place marker (pm) at beg of rnd. (The marker will be at the center front of the garment.) Join, being careful not to twist sts. With CC, k2 rnds. Beg working from graph and change to 29" needles when necessary. When graph is complete, work in MC and inc 0 (0, 4) sts, and dec 2 (4, 0) sts in first plain rnd: 378 (406, 434) sts. **Mark the Body and Sleeves:** Starting at the beg of the rnd, pm after: 58 (63, 68)

"The Large Collar" jacket.

sts for right front, 73 (77, 81) sts for right sleeve, 116 (126, 136) sts for back, and 73 (77, 81) sts for left sleeve. Work rem 58 (63, 68) sts for left front (4 markers in place). **Short Rows:** Short rows are worked to provide a better fit. They are basically used to lower the front neck and are worked back and forth in St st. Starting at beg of rnd, work to last marker (left sleeve marker); slip marker. Work 5 sts of left front. *Yarn forward; slip next st p-wise to right-hand needle. Yarn back, turn work. Slip first st back to right-hand needle (wrapped st). WS facing, purl to last marker (right sleeve marker); slip marker. P5 sts of right front; slip next st p-wise to right-hand needle. Yarn back; turn work. Slip first st back to right-hand needle. Yarn back (wrapped st). Knit to wrapped st of left front sts. Knit the wrap tog with the wrapped st, then k5 more sts of left front. Rep from*. Work 5 sts further into the front sts of the sweater on each side 4 times total (40 sts = 8 short rows). Beg working circularly again until yoke at center front meas 8 (9, 10)" or desired length from ribbing.

DIVIDE SLEEVES AND BODY: Sleeves: With larger needles and Looping Provisional Cast On, CO 2 sets of 24 (28, 32) sts for the underarms and set aside. With larger 29" circular needle, knit across 58 (63, 68) sts of right front, drop yarn and needle. **Join new ball of yarn and larger 16" circular needle. Knit across 73 (77, 81) sts of right sleeve, then across cast-on sts placing marker after 12th (14th, 16th) st: 97 (105, 113) sts. Join and work even for a total of 20 rnds, ending at marker. Dec rnd: *K1, k2tog, work

until 3 sts are left before marker, SSK, k1. Work 6 rnds even. Rep from* 16 (17, 18) more times: 63 (69, 75) sts. The sleeve is approximately 14½ (15¼, 16)" long. Change to dpn when necessary. Work 6 rnds even after last dec rnd. Final dec rnd: *K1, k2tog; rep from*: 42 (46, 50) sts. Change to smaller dpn. Work k1, p1 rib for 2–3". BO in pattern. At right underarm, pick up larger 29" circular needle with yarn attached, remove the waste yarn from right underarm sts, knit up 24 (28, 32) sts; knit across 116 (126, 136) back sts, then drop yarn and needle. Rep from** for left sleeve. **Body:** At left underarm, pick up larger 29" circular needle with yarn attached, remove the waste yarn from left underarm sts, knit up 24 (28, 32) sts; knit across rem 58 (63, 68) sts of left front: 280 (308, 336) sts. Continue working in the rnd until piece meas 14 (15, 16)" from underarm or desired length. Change to smaller needles. Work back and forth in k1, p1 rib for 2–3". BO in pattern. Baste down center front of sweater. Machine stitch twice on each side. Cut open.

BUTTONHOLE BAND: Beg at top of right front, using MC and rib needles, pick up the 8 sts of right Buttonhole Band from holder. *Work even in k1, p1 rib for approximately 3 (3¼, 3½)" from last buttonhole. With WS facing, rib 3 sts, work the One-Row Buttonhole (see page 74), rib to end. Rep from * 6 more times. Continue in k1, p1 rib for 1½ (1¾, 2)". Break yarn. Place sts on holder. The last buttonhole will be made in the bottom ribbing.

BUTTON BAND: Rep as for Buttonhole Band, omitting buttonholes, and do

not break yarn.

BOTTOM RIBBING: With rib needle and RS facing, pick up sts from left Button Band (make sure band is not twisted), body sts from waste yarn, and right Button Band sts (make sure band is not twisted). With MC attached at left Button Band, work back and forth in k1, p1 rib for 1½", end with RS. With WS facing, rib 3 sts, work the One-Row Buttonhole, rib to end. Work 1/2" of k1, p1 rib. BO in pattern.

FINISHING: Weave underarm seams. Sew Button and Buttonhole Bands to center fronts. Sew in ends. Sew on buttons.

THE LARGE COLLAR JACKET

Finished Sizes: 40 (44, 48)" approximate bust/chest width.

Materials: Kimmet Croft Fibers' Fairy Hare (60% Rambouillet wool, 40% Angora; 1 oz. = approx. 150 yards/137 meters): 8 (9, 10) oz. #FF46 (MC); 1 oz. Ang 5 (BB); 1 oz. each #FF24, #FF15, and #FF41; 1/2 oz. each #FF23, #FF19, #FF11, #FF40, and #FF44. Alice Starmore's Scottish Campion (100% pure Shetland wool; 1 oz. = approx. 150 yards/137 meters): 1 oz. #85 Mogit.
Nine 7/16" buttons.

Gauge: 7 sts and 10 rows equal 1" over St st. Adjust needle sizes if necessary to obtain the correct gauge (see page 69).

Needle Suggestions: Size 3 for unpatterned area; size 2 for patterned area; size 1 for bands.

RIGHT FRONT: With smallest nee-

JACKET

Work pattern repeat as given.

CARDIGAN

Rnd 9: inc 72 sts: 216 sts.
Rnd 26: inc 72 (90, 108) sts: 288 (306, 324) sts.
Rnd 45: inc 72 (102, 108) sts: 360 (408, 432) sts.
Rnd 59: inc 20 (0, 0) sts: 380 (408, 432) sts.
Rnd 64: inc 0 (2, 0) sts, and dec 0 (0, 2) sts: 380 (410, 430) sts.

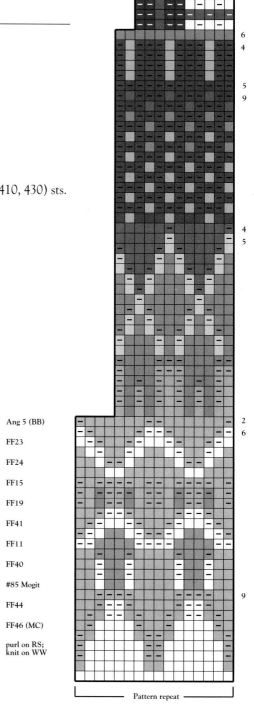

	Ang 5 (BB)
	FF23
	FF24
	FF15
	FF19
	FF41
	FF11
	FF40
	#85 Mogit
	FF44
	FF46 (MC)
−	purl on RS; knit on WW

Pattern repeat

dle and BB (band color), CO 154 (161, 168) sts. K6 rows. K16 sts, *work the One-Row Buttonhole (see page 74), k17 (18, 19) sts, rep from* 6 times total; work the One-Row Buttonhole, k15 (16, 17) sts. K5 rows (total of 6 garter st ridges). Change to medium needles and work 2 rows St st in BB color. Beg working from graph. Work even for 1½ (2, 2½)". Keeping in pattern, inc 1 st at neck edge (right side) 4 times, inc 2 sts once, inc 3 sts once, inc 5 sts once, inc 7 sts once: 175 (182, 189) sts. When graph is complete, work in MC until piece meas approximately 5¾ (6¼, 6¾)" from beg. RS facing, BO 62 (69, 76) sts for armhole. Work to end, p 1 row. RS facing, BO 2 sts at armhole edge 4 times: 105 sts rem (all sizes). This is the side seam and should meas approximately 15". Work even for 1". Piece should meas approximately 10½ (11, 11½)" from beg. BO rem 105 sts. With smallest needles and BB, pick up and k80 (85, 90) sts along bottom edge. K7 more rows. Next row: K74 (79, 84) sts, work One-Row Buttonhole, knit to end of row. K6 more rows. Using medium needle, BO on reverse side of knit (8 garter ridges).

LEFT FRONT: Work same as Right Front, reversing shaping and omitting buttonholes.

BACK: With largest needle and MC, CO 142 (156, 170) sts. Change to smallest needle. Work 1" in garter st. Change to largest needle. Work even in St st until piece meas 16" from beg. BO 2 sts at the beg of next 8 rows. Work until piece meas 26 (27, 28)" from beg. Place rem sts on 3 holders: 40 (44, 48) sts for each shoulder, and 46 (52, 58) sts for back.

SLEEVES: With largest needle and MC, CO 62 (70, 80) sts. Change to smallest needle. Work 1" in garter st. Change to largest needle and St st. Inc 6 (10, 12) sts evenly across next row: 68 (80, 92) sts. Inc 1 st each side every 4th row 31 (31, 32) times and every 6th row 5 (6, 6) times: 140 (154, 168) sts. Work even until piece meas 17½ (18, 18½)" from beg. BO 2 sts beg of next 8 rows. Place rem sts on holder.

FINISHING: Join shoulder seams. With smallest needle and BB, pick up and k45 (48, 50) sts from right center front to shoulder seam, 46 (52, 58) sts from back neck holder, 45 (48, 50) sts from shoulder seam to left center front: 136 (148, 158) sts. K3 more rows (2 garter ridges). On the next row dec 13 (16, 18) sts evenly across row. K1 more row. On next row, k3, work One-Row Buttonhole, knit to end of row. K1 more row. On next row dec 6 (9, 11) sts evenly across row: 117 (123, 129) sts. K3 more rows. Using medium needle, BO on reverse side in knit. BO or sew sleeves into armhole (see page 75). Sew side and sleeve seams.

THE POINT

Designed by Emma Jacobsson

THE POINT PULLOVER

Finished Size: 40 (42, 44, 46, 48)" approximate bust/chest width.

Materials: Kimmet Croft Fibers' Fairy Hare (60% Rambouillet wool, 40% Angora; 1 oz. = approx. 150 yards/137 meters): 7 (7½, 8, 8½, 9) oz. #FF 44 (MC). Alice Starmore's Scottish Campion (100% pure Shetland wool; 1 oz. = approx. 150 yards/137 meters): 1 skein #93 Natural (CC).

Gauge: 7 sts and 10 rows equal 1" over St st. Adjust needle sizes if necessary to obtain the correct gauge (see page 69).

Needle Suggestions: Size 3 for body and sleeves; size 2 for ribbing—straight and 16" circular.

BACK: With MC and smaller needles, CO 133 (141, 147, 155, 161) sts. Work k1, p1 rib for 3". Change to larger needles and St st. Inc 1 st each side every 1", 4 times: 141 (149, 155, 163, 169) sts. Work even in St st until piece meas 13½ (14, 14½, 15, 15½)" from beg. BO 2 sts at beg of next 8 rows: 125 (133, 139, 147, 153) sts rem. Work even until piece meas

■ Sz 40
■ Sz 42
■ Sz 44
□ Sz 46
■ Sz 48
□ #93 Natural (CC)
■ FF44 (MC)
⊟ purl on RS;
   knit on WS

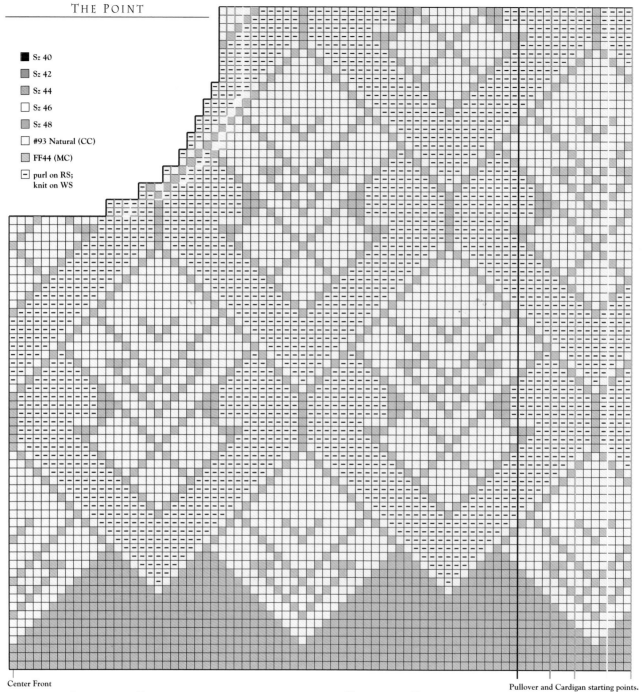

Center Front

Pullover and Cardigan starting points.

CARDIGAN FRONTS

Dec 1 more st at each neck edge (1 (1, 0, 1, 1) time:
37 (40, 42, 45, 47) sts.

PULLOVER FRONT

Beg at appropriate starting point and work to center st.
Work back to starting point.

23½ (24½, 25½, 26½, 27½)" from beg. Divide sts onto 3 holders: 37 (40, 42, 45, 47) sts for each shoulder, and 51 (53, 55, 57, 59) sts for back neck.

FRONT: With MC and smaller needles, CO 133 (141, 147, 155, 161) sts. Work k1, p1 rib for 3". Change to larger needles and St st. Inc 1 st each side every 1", 4 times: 141 (149, 155, 163, 169) sts. Work even until piece meas 13½ (14, 14½, 15, 15½)" from beg. BO 2 sts at beg of next 8 rows: 125 (133, 139, 147, 153) sts rem. Work even until piece meas 15½ (16½, 17½, 18½, 19½)" from beg. Follow graph instructions starting at point indicated for appropriate size. Work even until piece meas 21 (22, 23, 24, 25)" from beg. Work neckline shaping according to graph. Work even until piece meas 23½ (24½, 25½, 26½, 27½)" from beg. Place rem shoulder sts on holder.

SLEEVES: With smaller needles and MC, CO 63 (67, 71, 75, 79) sts. Work k1, p1 rib for 3" ending on RS row. WS facing, purl across inc 7 (9, 11, 13, 15) sts evenly spaced: 70 (76, 82, 88, 94) sts. Change to larger needles and St st. Inc 1 st each side every 4th row 30 (31, 31, 31, 31) times, then every 6th row 5 (5, 5, 6, 6) times: 140 (148, 154, 162, 168) sts. Work even until sleeve meas 17 (17½, 17½, 18, 18)" from beg. BO 2 sts at the beg of next 8 rows. Place rem 124 (132, 138, 146, 152) sts on holder.

FINISHING: With RS facing, BO fronts and back tog at shoulder seam (see page 75). Starting at the left shoulder seam, with MC and circular needle, pick up and knit 24 sts along left neck edge, 23 (25, 27, 29, 31) sts from front holder, 24

sts along right neck edge, and 51 (53, 53, 57, 59) sts from back holder: 122 (126, 130, 134, 138) sts. Work k1, p1 rib for 1". BO in pattern. BO sleeves onto the body (see page 75). Sew side and sleeve seams.

THE POINT CARDIGAN

Finished Size: 40 (42, 44, 46, 48)" approximate bust/chest width.

Materials: Kimmet Croft Fibers' Fairy Hare (60% Rambouillet wool, 40% Angora; 1 oz. = approx. 150 yards/137 meters): 6½ (7, 7½, 8, 8½) oz. #FF 44 (MC). Alice Starmore's Scottish Campion (100% pure Shetland wool; 1 oz. = approx. 150 yards/137 meters): 1 skein #93 Natural (CC).
Seven 7/16" buttons.

Gauge: 7 sts and 10 rows equal 1" over St st. Adjust needle sizes if necessary to obtain the correct gauge (see page 69).

Needle Suggestions: Size 3 for body and sleeves; size 2 for ribbing.

BACK: With MC and smaller needles, CO 133 (141, 147, 155, 161) sts. Work k1, p1 rib for 1". Change to larger needles and St st. Inc 1 st each side every 1", 4 times: 141 (149, 155, 163, 169) sts. Work even until piece meas 10½ (11, 11, 11½, 11½)" from beg. BO 2 sts at beg of next 8 rows: 125 (133, 139, 147, 153) sts rem. Work even until piece meas 20½ (21½, 22, 23, 23½)" from beg. Divide sts onto 3 holders: 37 (40, 42, 45, 47) sts for each shoulder, and 51 (53, 55, 57, 59) sts for back neck.

LEFT FRONT: With MC and smaller needles, CO 74 (78, 81, 85, 88) sts. Work

k1 p1 rib for 1". With WS facing, rib 7 sts and place on holder (Button Band): 67 (71, 74, 78, 81) sts rem. Change to larger needles and St st. Inc 1 st at side seam every 1", 4 times: 71 (75, 78, 82, 85) sts. Work even until piece meas 10½ (11, 11, 11½, 11½)" from beg. BO 2 sts at armhole edge 4 times: 63 (67, 70, 74, 77) sts rem. Work even until piece meas 12½ (13½, 14, 15, 15½)" from beg, ending on right side row. Follow graph instructions starting at point indicated for appropriate size. Work neckline shaping according to graph. Keeping in pattern, work until piece meas 20½ (21½, 22, 23, 23½)" from beg. Place rem shoulder sts on holder.

RIGHT FRONT: Work as for Left Front reversing shaping and working buttonholes as follows: Work k1 p1 rib for 1/2". With RS facing, rib 2 sts, work One-Row Buttonhole (see page 74), rib to end. Work even in rib for 1/2" more. With RS facing, rib 7 sts and place on holder (Buttonhole Band). Work even until piece meas 12½ (13½, 14, 15, 15½)" from beg, ending on wrong side row.

SLEEVES: With smaller needles and MC, CO 63 (67, 71, 75, 79) sts. Work k1, p1 rib for 1" ending on RS row. WS facing, purl across inc 7 (9, 11, 13, 15) sts evenly: 70 (76, 82, 88, 94) sts. Change to larger needles and St st. Inc 1 st each side every 4th row 30 (31, 31, 31, 31) times, then every 6th row 5 (5, 5, 6, 6) times: 140 (148, 154, 162, 168) sts. Work even until sleeve meas 17 (17½, 17½, 18, 18)" from beg. BO 2 sts at the beg of next 8 rows. Place rem 124 (132, 138, 146, 152) sts on holder.

BUTTON BANDS: Right: With smaller needles and MC, pick up the 7 sts of right Buttonhole Band from holder. *Work even in k1, p1 rib for approximately 2¾ (3, 3, 3¼, 3⅓)" from last buttonhole. With the RS facing, rib 2 sts, work the One-Row Buttonhole, rib to end. Rep from* 4 more times. Continue in k1, p1 rib for 2¼ (2½, 2½, 2¾, 2¾)". Do not break yarn. Place sts on holder. The last buttonhole will be worked in the neckband. Left: Rep as for right Button Band, omitting buttonholes and breaking yarn.

FINISHING: BO fronts and back tog at shoulder seam (see page 75). With smaller needles, RS facing, and MC attached, rib 7 sts of right Buttonhole Band from holder, pick up and knit 35 (35, 37, 37, 39) sts along right neck edge, 51 (53, 55, 57, 59) sts from back holder, 35 (35, 37, 37, 39) sts along left neck edge, rib 7 sts of left Button Band from holder: 135 (137, 143, 145, 151) sts. Work k1, p1 rib for 1/2", work the One-Row Buttonhole at neckline on right front band. Work an additional 1/2" of k1, p1 rib. BO in pattern. Sew Button Bands to center front edges. BO sleeves onto the body (see page 75). Sew side and sleeve seams. Sew on buttons.

THE CHINESE

❧ Designed by Emma Jacobsson ❧

THE CHINESE PULLOVER

Finished Size: 40 (42, 44, 46, 48)" approximate bust/chest width.

Materials: Jamieson & Smith's 2 Ply Jumper Weight (100% pure Shetland wool; 1 oz. = approx. 150 yards/137 meters): 11 (12, 12, 12, 13) skeins #202 Beige (MC); 2 (3, 3, 3, 3) skeins #4 Moorit (CC).

Gauge: 7 sts and 10 rows equal 1" over St st. Adjust needle sizes if necessary to obtain the correct gauge (see page 69).

Needle Suggestions: Size 3 for body and sleeves; size 2 for ribbing—straight and 16" circular.

BACK: With MC and smaller needles, CO 125 (133, 139, 147, 153) sts. Work k1, p1 rib for 3" ending on RS row. WS facing, purl across inc 14 sts evenly spaced: 139 (147, 153, 161, 167) sts. Change to larger needles and St st. Work

even in St st until piece meas 13½ (14, 14½, 15, 15½)" from beg. BO 2 sts at beg of next 8 rows: 123 (131, 137, 145, 151) sts rem. Work even until piece meas 23½ (24½, 25½, 26½, 27½)" from beg. Divide sts onto 3 holders: 36 (39, 41, 44, 46) sts for each shoulder, and 51 (53, 55, 57, 59) sts for back neck.

FRONT: With MC and smaller needles, CO 125 (133, 139, 147, 153) sts. Work k1, p1 rib for 3" ending on RS row. WS facing, purl across inc 13 sts evenly spaced: 138 (146, 152, 160, 166) sts. Change to larger needles. Follow graph instructions. Work even in established pattern until piece meas 13½ (14, 14½, 15, 15½)" from beg. BO 2 sts at beg of next 8 rows: 122 (130, 136, 144, 150) sts rem. Work even until piece meas 21 (22, 23, 24, 25)" from beg. **Shape neck:** Keeping in pattern, work 47 (50, 52, 55, 57) sts, place center 28 (30, 32, 34, 36) sts on holder. Attach new balls of yarn, work rem 47 (50, 52, 55, 57) sts. Keeping in pattern and working both sides at the same time, BO from each neck edge 4 sts once, 3 sts once, 2 sts once, then dec 1 st twice: 36 (39, 41, 44, 46) sts rem. Keeping in pattern, work even until piece meas 23½ (24½, 25½, 26½, 27½)" from beg. Place rem shoulder sts on holder.

SLEEVES: With smaller needles and MC, CO 63 (67, 71, 75, 79) sts. Work k1, p1 rib for 3" ending on RS row. WS facing, purl across inc 7 (9, 11, 13, 15) sts evenly spaced: 70 (76, 82, 88, 94) sts. Change to larger needles and St st. Inc 1 st each side every 4th row 30 (31, 31, 31, 31) times, then every 6th row 5 (5, 5, 6, 6) times: 140 (148, 154, 162, 168) sts.

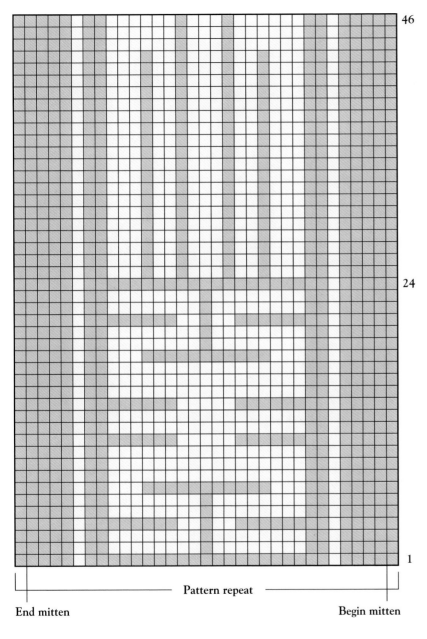

46

24

1

Pattern repeat

End mitten

Begin mitten

 #4 Moorit (CC) ☐ #202 Beige (MC)

MITTEN

Begin as indicated.
Row 1: inc 1 st on needle 1: 16 sts.
Follow pattern as marked.
Work rnds 1–46, then rnds 1–24: 70 rnds.
On second rnd 24: dec 1 st on needle 1: 15 sts.

PULLOVER

K3 (7, 10, 14, 17) sts in MC; rep graph 4
times; end k3 (7, 10, 14, 17) sts in MC.

CARDIGAN

Right Front: Beginning at center front, work
pattern repeat twice, then with MC, k2 (6, 8,
12, 16) sts.
Left Front: Beginning at side edge and MC, k2
(6, 8, 12, 16) sts, then work pattern repeat
twice.

Work even until sleeve meas 17 (17½, 17½, 18, 18)" from beg. BO 2 sts at the beg of next 8 rows. Place rem 124 (132, 138, 146, 152) sts on holder.

FINISHING: BO fronts and back tog at shoulder seam (see page 75). Starting at the left shoulder seam, with MC and circular needle, pick up and knit 25 sts along left neck edge, 28 (30, 32, 34, 36) sts from front holder, 24 sts along right neck edge, and 51 (53, 55, 57, 59) sts from back holder: 128 (132, 136, 140, 144) sts. Work k1, p1 rib for 1". BO in pattern. BO sleeves onto the body (see page 75). Sew side and sleeve seams.

THE CHINESE CARDIGAN

Finished Size: 40 (42, 44, 46, 48)" approximate bust/chest width.

Materials: Jamieson & Smith's 2 Ply Jumper Weight (100% pure Shetland wool; 1 oz. = approx. 150 yards/137 meters): 11 (11, 12, 12, 12) skeins #202 Beige (MC); 2 (2, 3, 3, 3) skeins #4 Moorit (CC).
Seven 7/16" buttons.

Gauge: 7 sts and 10 rows equal 1" over St st. Adjust needle sizes if necessary to obtain the correct gauge (see page 69).

Needle Suggestions: Size 3 for body and sleeves; size 2 for ribbing—straight and 16" circular.

BACK: With MC and smaller needles, CO 133 (141, 147, 155, 161) sts. Work k1, p1 rib for 1". Change to larger needles and St st. Inc 1 st each side every 1", 4 times: 141 (149, 155, 163, 169) sts. Work even until piece meas 10½ (11, 11,

11½, 11½)" from beg. BO 2 sts at beg of next 8 rows: 125 (133, 139, 147, 153) sts rem. Work even until piece meas 20½ (21½, 22, 23, 23½)" from beg. Divide sts onto 3 holders: 38 (42, 44, 47, 49) sts for each shoulder, and 49 (49, 51, 53, 55) sts for back neck.

RIGHT FRONT: With MC and smaller needles, CO 75 (79, 81, 85, 89) sts. Work k1, p1 rib for 1/2". With RS facing, rib 2 sts, work the One-Row Buttonhole (see page 74), rib to end. Work even in rib for 1". With RS facing, rib 7 sts and place on holder (Buttonhole Band): 68 (72, 74, 78, 82) sts rem. Change to larger needles and St st. Follow graph instructions, and at the same time, inc 1 st at side seam every 1", 4 times: 72, (76, 78, 82, 86) sts. Work even until piece meas 10½ (11, 11, 11½, 11½)" from beg ending with a RS row. With WS facing, BO 2 sts at armhole edge 4 times: 64 (68, 70, 74, 78) sts rem. Work even until piece meas 18 (19, 19½, 20½, 21)" from beg ending with a WS row. **Shape neck:** At neck edge, keeping in pattern, BO 14 (14, 14, 15, 17) sts once, 4 sts once, 2 sts twice, then dec 1 st every other row 4 times: 38 (42, 44, 47, 49) sts rem. Keeping in pattern, work even until piece meas 20½ (21½, 22, 23, 23½)" from beg. Place rem shoulder sts on holder.

LEFT FRONT: Work as for Right Front reversing shaping and omitting buttonhole in bottom ribbing.

SLEEVES: With smaller needles and MC, CO 63 (67, 71, 75, 79) sts. Work k1, p1 rib for 1" ending on RS row. WS facing, purl across inc 7 (9, 11, 13, 15) sts evenly: 70 (76, 82, 88, 94) sts. Change to

larger needles and St st. Inc 1 st each side every 4th row 30 (31, 31, 31, 31) times, then every 6th row 5 (5, 5, 6, 6) times: 140 (148, 154, 162, 168) sts. Work even until sleeve meas 17 (17½, 17½, 18, 18)" from beg. BO 2 sts at the beg of next 8 rows. Place rem 124 (132, 138, 146, 152) sts on holder.

BUTTON BANDS: Right: With smaller needles and MC, pick up the 7 sts of right Buttonhole Band from holder. *Work even in k1, p1 rib for approximately 2¾ (3, 3, 3¼, 3⅓)" from last buttonhole. With RS facing, rib 2 sts, work the One-Row Buttonhole, rib to end. Rep from* 4 more times. Continue in k1, p1 rib for 2¼ (2½, 2½, 2¾, 2¾)". Do not break yarn. Place sts on holder. The last buttonhole will be made in the neckband. **Left:** Rep as for right Button Band, omitting buttonholes and breaking yarn.

FINISHING: BO fronts and back tog at shoulder seam (see page 75). With smaller needles, RS facing, and MC attached, rib 7 sts of right Buttonhole Band from holder, pick up and knit 35 (35, 37, 37, 39) sts along right neck edge, 49 (49, 51, 53, 55) sts from back holder, 35 (35, 37, 37, 39) sts along left neck edge, rib 7 sts of left Button Band from holder: 133 (133, 139, 141, 147) sts. Work k1, p1 rib for 1/2", work the One-Row Buttonhole at neckline on right front band. Work an additional 1/2" of k1, p1 rib. BO in pattern. Sew Button Bands to center front edges. BO sleeves onto the body (see page 75). Sew side and sleeve seams. Sew on buttons.

Finished Size: Women's.

Materials: Jamieson & Smith's 2 Ply Jumper Weight (100% pure Shetland wool; 1 oz. = approx. 150 yards/137 meters): 1 oz. #202 Beige (MC); 1/2 oz. #4 Moorit.

Gauge: 7 sts and 10 rows equal 1" over St st. Adjust needle sizes if necessary to obtain the correct gauge (see page 69).

Needle Suggestions: Size 2 double pointed (set of five).

CUFF: (Select desired style.) **Reverse St st cuff:** With MC, CO 60 sts. Divide evenly between 4 needles (15 sts per needle). Join, being careful not to twist sts. Work even in St st for 2¹/₂". Turn cuff inside out, so the reverse St st becomes the right side. The needle where the yarn end is located is needle 1. The other needles are numbered clockwise from needle 1. With yarn in back, slip one st from needle 4 to needle 1, bring yarn forward, slip st back to needle 4. You have worked a turn st which will prevent a hole in the cuff. K1 rnd, dec 6 sts evenly: 60 sts. Work one rnd even. K1 rnd, inc 6 sts evenly. Continue at Mitten Body. **Rib cuff:** With MC, CO 54 sts. Divide between 4 needles (13, 14, 13, 14 sts per needle). Join, being careful not to twist sts. Work in k1, p1 rib for 3". Work one rnd in St st inc 6 sts evenly: 60 sts. Continue at Mitten Body. **Note:** 1. Needles 1 and 2 hold the palm sts for the mitten and are worked in MC. Needles 3 and 4 hold the patterned, back side of the mitten and are worked in multiple colors following graph. 2. Follow graph making increases or decreases

in rounds indicated. This is necessary to make the sts in the round evenly divisible by the number of sts in the pattern repeat. 3. The cuff and mitten top are worked in the round in MC. The patterned portion of the mitten is worked back and forth in St st in multiple colors (see Mitten Body).

MITTEN BODY: Right Hand: Starting with needle 1, k1, p1, k3, place marker, p1, k9. Knit across needle 2. Leave yarn at the end of needle 2. Go to needle 4 and attach a second ball of MC. Turn work. Purl across needles 4 and 3. Twist the yarn ends between needles 2 and 3 to close the side of the mitten. The patterned side of the mitten will be facing you. Work Row 1 of chart. Purl across needles 2 and 1. Twist the yarn ends between needles 1 and 4 to close the other side of the mitten. The palm of the mitten is always worked in MC. Continue working back and forth, twisting the yarn at row ends. At the same time, on the palm side work a thumb gusset by inc 1 st every knit row before the marker, 12 times. After the final thumb gusset inc row, twist yarns at end of row and purl back to marker. Place 17 sts after marker on a holder. CO 6 sts at end of purl row: 15 sts on needle 1. Work even in St st until graph is completed. **Shape Mitten Top:** With MC and starting at needle 1, k2 rnds. *K1, SSK, knit to last 3 sts on needle 2, k2tog, k1. Then, k1, SSK, knit to last 3 sts on needle 4, K2tog, K1. Rep from* until 8 sts rem. Draw yarn through sts and tighten to end off. **Thumb:** Put 17 sts on holder onto one dpn. Knit across 8 sts on needle 1, knit across next 8 sts

for needle 2, knit rem st onto needle 3 and pick up and knit 7 sts along the CO sts. There will be a total of 24 sts, 8 per needle. Working in the rnd, work even in St st for 28 rnds. In the next rnd, k2tog across rnd: 12 sts rem. In the next rnd, k2tog across rnd: 6 sts rem. Draw yarn through sts and tighten to end off. **Left Hand:** After the cuff is worked, knit across needle 1, k9 sts on needle 2, p1, place marker, k3, p1, k1. Continue to work the same as Right Hand.

FINISHING: Sew in ends. For the reverse St st cuff, if desired, brush cuff with a stiff brush (such as a vegetable brush) to raise the nap.

THE SHIELD

✖ *Designed by Annika Malmström-Bladini* ✖

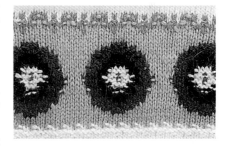

THE SHIELD YOKE PULLOVER

Finished Size: 40 (44, 48)" approximate bust/chest width.

Materials: Kimmet Croft Fibers' Fairy Hare (60% Rambouillet wool, 40% Angora; 1 oz. = approx. 150 yards/137 meters): 9 (10, 11) oz. Ang 5 (MC);

CAP

Work even in pattern repeat as given.

PULLOVER AND CARDIGAN

Rnd 7: inc 72 sts: 216 sts.

Rnd 27: inc 72 (108, 108) sts: 288 (324, 324) sts.

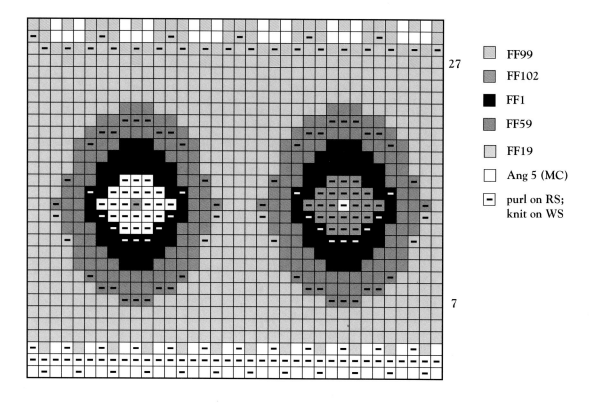

▨	**FF99**
▩	**FF102**
■	**FF1**
▦	**FF59**
▢	**FF19**
☐	**Ang 5 (MC)**
▬	**purl on RS; knit on WS**

1/2 oz. #FF19; 1/3 oz. #FF59 and #FF1; 1/4 oz. each #FF99, and #FF102.

Gauge: 7 sts and 10 rows equal 1" over St st. Adjust needle sizes if necessary to obtain the correct gauge (see page 69).

Needle Suggestions: Size 3 for unpatterned areas—16" and 29" circular, and double pointed; size 2 for patterned areas—16" and 29" circular, and double pointed; size 1 for ribbing—29" circular, and double pointed.

Note: Follow graph making increases or decreases in rounds indicated. This is necessary to make the sts in the round evenly divisible by the number of sts in the pattern repeat.

YOKE: (All Sizes) With MC, smaller needle, and using the Looping Provisional Cast On (see page 70), CO 120 sts. Place marker (pm) at beg of rnd. (The marker will be at the back of the right shoulder on the garment.) Join, being careful not to twist sts. With MC, work 2" in k1, p1 rib. (Later, the ribbing will be folded in half to the inside of the neckline, the waste yarn will be removed, and the live sts stitched in place. This allows for plenty of give in the neck.) K1 rnd MC, inc 24 sts evenly: 144 sts. Beg working from graph. When graph is complete change to larger needles. Work in MC until yoke meas 5" from beg of colorwork after ribbing. Inc 90 (82, 110) sts evenly in next rnd: 378 (406, 434) sts. **Mark the Body and Sleeves:** Starting at the beg of the rnd, pm after: 116 (126, 136) sts for back, 73 (77, 81) sts for left sleeve, 116 (126, 136) sts for front, and 73 (77, 81) sts for right sleeve (4 markers in place). Break yarn. **Short Rows:** Short rows are worked to provide a better fit. They are basically used to lower the front neck and are worked back and forth in St st. Starting at beg of round (back of the right shoulder), sl sts of right sleeve, right front marker and 6 sts of right front to left-hand side of needle. With RS facing, join new yarn. Keeping tail at back of work, bring yarn from back to front between needle tips, sl first st on left-hand side of needle to right-hand side, yarn back (wrapped st). K5 sts of right front, sl marker, work to 5 sts beyond last marker (5 sts of left front worked). Continue with short rows: *Yarn forward; slip next st p-wise to right-hand needle. Yarn back; turn work. Slip first st back to right-hand needle (wrapped st). WS facing, purl to last marker (right front marker); slip marker, purl to the wrapped st, purl the wrap tog with the wrapped st on the needle, p5 more sts of right front; slip next st p-wise to right-hand needle. Yarn back; turn work. Slip first st back to right-hand needle. Yarn back (wrapped st). Knit to wrapped st of left front. Knit the wrap tog with the wrapped st on the needle, then k5 more sts of left front. Rep from*. Work 5 sts further into the front sts of the sweater on each side 4 times total (40 sts = 8 short rows) ending at left front. Beg working circularly again until yoke at center front meas 8 (9, 10)" (measured straight up) or desired length from the beg of the colorwork after the ribbing. End at back of the right shoulder marker.

DIVIDE SLEEVES AND BODY: Sleeves: With larger needles and Looping Provisional Cast On, CO 2 sets of 24 (28, 32) sts for the underarms and set aside. With larger 29" circular needle, knit across 116 (126, 136) back sts, drop yarn and needle. **Join new ball of yarn and larger 16" circular needle. Knit across 73 (77, 81) sts of left sleeve, then across cast-on sts placing marker after 12th (14th, 16th) st: 97 (105, 113) sts. Join and work even for a total of 20 rnds, ending at marker. Dec rnd: *K1, k2tog, work until 3 sts are left before marker, SSK, k1. Work 6 rnds even. Rep from* 16 (17, 18) more times: 63 (69, 75) sts rem. The sleeve is approximately 14½ (15¼, 16)" long. Change to dpn when necessary. Work 6 rnds even after last dec rnd. Final dec rnd: *K1, k2tog; rep from*: 42 (46, 50) sts rem. Change to smaller dpn. Work k1, p1 rib for 2–3". BO in pattern. At left underarm, pick up larger 29" circular needle with yarn attached, remove the waste yarn from left underarm sts, knit up 24 (28, 32) sts; knit across 116 (126, 136) front sts, then drop yarn and needle. Rep from** for right sleeve. **Body:** At right underarm, pick up larger 29" circular needle with yarn attached, remove the waste yarn from right underarm sts, knit up 24 (28, 32) sts: 280 (308, 336) sts. Continue working in the rnd until desired length from neck rib less body rib length. Change to smaller dpn. Work in k1, p1 rib for 2–3". BO in pattern.

FINISHING: Weave underarm seams. Sew in ends. Fold neck ribbing in half to inside. Remove waste yarn and st in place.

Finished Size: 40 (44, 48)" approximate bust/chest width.

Materials: Kimmet Croft Fibers' Fairy Hare (60% Rambouillet wool, 40% Angora; 1 oz. = approx. 150 yards/137 meters): 9 (10, 11) oz. Ang 5 (MC); 1/2 oz. #FF19; 1/3 oz. #FF59 and #FF1; 1/4 oz. each #FF99, and #FF102. Nine 5/8" buttons.

Gauge: 7 sts and 10 rows equal 1" over St st. Adjust needle sizes if necessary to obtain the correct gauge (see page 69).

Needle Suggestions: Size 3 for unpatterned areas—16" and 29" circular; size 2 for patterned areas—16" and 29" circular, and double pointed; size 1 for ribbing—29" circular, and double pointed.

Note: Follow graph making increases or decreases in rounds indicated. This is necessary in order to make the sts in the round evenly divisible by the number of sts in the pattern repeat.

YOKE: (All Sizes) With MC and rib needle, CO 121 sts. Work back and forth in k1, p1 rib for 1/2". With RS facing, rib 3 sts, work the One-Row Buttonhole (see page 74), rib to end. Work k1, p1 rib for 1/2", ending on RS row. With WS facing, work 8 rib sts and place on holder (left Button Band), purl 105 sts, at the same time inc 39 sts evenly, rib rem 8 sts. With RS facing, rib 8 sts and place on holder (right Buttonhole Band): 144 sts rem. Place marker (pm) at beg of rnd. (The marker will be at the center front of the garment.) Join, being careful not to twist sts. With MC, k2 rnds. Beg working from

graph and change to 29" needles when necessary. When graph is complete, there will be 288 (324, 324) sts. Change to larger needles. Work even in MC for 2 rnd. On next rnd, increase 90 (82, 110) sts evenly: 378 (406, 434) sts. **Mark the Body and Sleeves:** Starting at the beg of the rnd, pm after: 58 (63, 68) sts for right front, 73 (77, 81) sts for right sleeve, 116 (126, 136) sts for back, and 73 (77, 81) sts for left sleeve. Work rem 58 (63, 68) sts for left front (4 markers in place).

Short Rows: Short rows are worked to provide a better fit. They are basically used to lower the front neck and are worked back and forth in St st. Starting at beg of rnd, work to last marker (left sleeve marker); slip marker. Work 5 sts of left front. *Yarn forward; slip next st p-wise to right-hand needle. Yarn back, turn work. Slip first st back to right-hand needle (wrapped st). WS facing, purl to last marker (right sleeve marker); slip marker. P5 sts of right front; slip next st p-wise to right-hand needle. Yarn back; turn work. Slip first st back to right-hand needle. Yarn back (wrapped st). Knit to wrapped st of left front sts. Knit the wrap tog with the wrapped st, then k5 more sts of left front. Rep from*. Work 5 sts further into the front sts of the sweater on each side 4 times total (40 sts = 8 short rows). Beg working circularly again until yoke at center front meas 8 (9, 10)" or desired length from beg of colorwork.

DIVIDE SLEEVES AND BODY: Sleeves: With larger needles and Looping Provisional Cast On, CO 2 sets of 24 (28, 32) sts for the underarms and set aside. With larger 29" circular needle, knit

across 58 (63, 68) sts of right front, drop yarn and needle. ****Join new ball of yarn and larger 16" circular needle. Knit across 73 (77, 81) sts of right sleeve, then across cast-on sts placing marker after 12th (14th, 16th) st: 97 (105, 113) sts. Join and work even for a total of 20 rnds, ending at marker. Dec rnd: *K1, k2tog, work until 3 sts are left before marker, SSK, k1. Work 6 rnds even. Rep from* 16 (17, 18) more times: 63 (69, 75) sts. The sleeve is approximately 14 1/2 (15 1/4, 16)" long. Change to dpn when necessary. Work 6 rnds even after last dec rnd. Final dec rnd: *K1, k2tog; rep from*: 42 (46, 50) sts. Change to smaller dpn. Work k1, p1 rib for 2–3". BO in pattern. At right underarm, pick up larger 29" circular needle with yarn attached, remove the waste yarn from right underarm sts, knit up 24 (28, 32) sts; knit across 116 (126, 136) back sts, then drop yarn and needle. Rep from** for left sleeve. **Body:** At left underarm, pick up larger 29" circular needle with yarn attached, remove the waste yarn from left underarm sts, knit up 24 (28, 32) sts; knit across rem 58 (63, 68) sts of left front: 280 (308, 336) sts. Continue working in the rnd until piece meas 14 (15, 16)" from underarm or desired length. BO 4 sts at center front. Baste down center front of sweater. Machine stitch twice on each side. Cut open.

BUTTONHOLE BAND: Beg at top of right front, using MC and rib needles, pick up the 8 sts of right Buttonhole Band from holder. *Work even in k1, p1 rib for approximately 3 (3 1/4, 3 1/2)" from last buttonhole. With WS facing, rib 3 sts, work the One-Row Buttonhole (see page 74), rib to end. Rep from * 6 more times. Continue in k1, p1 rib for 1½ (1¾, 2)". Break yarn. Place sts on holder. The last buttonhole will be made in the bottom ribbing.

BUTTON BAND: Rep as for Buttonhole Band, omitting buttonholes, and do not break yarn.

BOTTOM RIBBING: With rib needle and RS facing, pick up sts from left Button Band (make sure band is not twisted), body sts from waste yarn, and right Button Band sts (make sure band is not twisted). With MC attached at left Button Band, work back and forth in k1, p1 rib for 1½", end with RS. With WS facing, rib 3 sts, work the One-Row Buttonhole, rib to end. Work 1/2" of k1, p1 rib. BO in pattern.

FINISHING: Weave underarm seams.

Sew button and Buttonhole Bands to center fronts. Sew in ends. Sew on buttons.

THE SHIELD CAP

Finished Size: 23" circumference.

Materials: Kimmet Croft Fibers' Fairy Hare (60% Rambouillet wool, 40% Angora; 1 oz. = approx. 150 yards/137 meters): 1 oz. Ang 5 (MC); 1/4 oz. each #FF99, #FF102, #FF19, #FF59, and #FF1.

Gauge: 7 sts and 10 rows equal 1" over St st. Adjust needle sizes if necessary to obtain the correct gauge (see page 69).

Needle Suggestions: size 2 for patterned area—6" circular, and double pointed; size 1 for ribbing—16" circular.

With MC and smaller needle, CO 146. Place marker at beg of rnd. Join, being careful not to twist sts. Work 3/4" in k1, p1 rib. Change to larger needle, work 1 rnd, inc 16 sts evenly: 162 sts. Work even following graph. After completing graph, work even in MC until piece meas approximately 7" from beg. With MC, work 1 rnd, dec 1 st evenly: 161 sts. **Seven Point Crown:** Begin working with circular needles and change to dpn when necessary. Work dbl dec at seven points as follows: sl 2 sts k-wise tog, k1, p2sso. *Rnd 1:* *K20, dbl dec; rep from* 6 times. *Rnd 2 and even numbered rnds:* Knit. *Rnd 3:* *K18 dbl dec; rep from* 6 times. Continue in this manner, working 1 less st before and after each dbl dec until 21 sts rem. Work dbl dec around: 7 sts rem. Draw yarn through 7 sts. Sew in ends.

THE AXES

❧ Designed by Emma Jacobsson ❧

THE AXES PULLOVER

Finished Size: 40 (42, 44, 46, 48)" approximate bust/chest width.

Materials: Jamieson & Smith's 2 Ply Jumper Weight (100% pure Shetland wool; 1 oz. = approx. 150 yards/137 meters): 11 (12, 12, 12, 13) skeins #202 Beige (MC); 2 (3, 3, 3, 3) skeins #4 Moorit.

Gauge: 7 sts and 10 rows equal 1" over St st. Adjust needle sizes if necessary to obtain the correct gauge (see page 69).

Needle Suggestions: Size 3 for body and sleeves; size 2 for ribbing—straight and 16" circular.

BACK: With MC and smaller needles, CO 125 (133, 139, 147, 153) sts. Work k1, p1 rib for 3" ending on RS row. WS facing, purl across inc 14 sts evenly spaced: 139 (147, 153, 161, 167) sts. Change to larger needles and St st. Work even in St st until piece meas 13½ (14, 14½, 15, 15½)" from beg. BO 2 sts at beg of next 8 rows: 123 (131, 137, 145, 151) sts rem. Work even until piece meas 23½ (24½, 25½, 26½, 27½)" from beg. Divide sts onto 3 holders: 36 (39, 41, 44, 46) sts for each shoulder, and 51 (53, 55, 57, 59) sts for back neck.

FRONT: With MC and smaller needles, CO 125 (133, 139, 147, 153) sts. Work k1, p1 rib for 3" ending on RS row. WS facing, purl across inc 14 sts evenly spaced: 139 (147, 153, 161, 167) sts.

Change to larger needles. Follow graph instructions starting at point indicated for appropriate size. Work even in established pattern until piece meas 13½ (14, 14½, 15, 15½)" from beg. BO 2 sts at beg of next 8 rows: 123 (131, 137, 145, 151) sts rem. Work even until piece meas 21 (22, 23, 24, 25)" from beg. **Shape neck:** Keeping in pattern, work 47 (50, 52, 55, 57) sts, place center 29 (31, 33, 35, 37) sts on holder. Attach new balls of yarn, work rem 47 (50, 52, 55, 57) sts. Keeping in pattern and working both sides at the same time, BO from each neck edge 4 sts once, 3 sts once, 2 sts once, then dec 1 st twice: 36 (39, 41, 44, 46) sts rem. Keeping in pattern, work even until piece meas 23½ (24½, 25½, 26½, 27½)" from beg. Place rem shoulder sts on holder.

SLEEVES: With smaller needles and MC, CO 63 (67, 71, 75, 79) sts. Work k1, p1 rib for 3" ending on RS row. WS facing, purl across inc 7 (9, 11, 13, 15) sts evenly spaced: 70 (76, 82, 88, 94) sts. Change to larger needles and St st. Inc 1 st each side every 4th row 30 (31, 31, 31, 31) times, then every 6th row 5 (5, 5, 6, 6) times: 140 (148, 154, 162, 168) sts. Work even until sleeve meas 17 (17½, 17½, 18, 18)" from beg. BO 2 sts at the beg of next 8 rows. Place rem 124 (132, 138, 146, 152) sts on holder.

FINISHING: BO fronts and back tog at shoulder seam (see page 75). Starting at the left shoulder seam, with MC and circular needle, pick up and knit 24 sts along left neck edge, 29 (31, 33, 35, 37) sts from front holder, 24 sts along right neck edge, and 51 (53, 55, 57, 59) sts from back holder: 128 (132, 136, 140,

144) sts. Work k1, p1 rib for 1". BO in pattern. BO sleeves onto the body (see page 75). Sew side and sleeve seams.

THE AXES CARDIGAN

Finished Size: 40 (42, 44, 46, 48)" approximate bust/chest width.

Materials: Jamieson & Smith's 2 Ply Jumper Weight (100% pure Shetland wool; 1 oz. = approx. 150 yards/137 meters): 11 (11, 12, 12, 12) skeins #202 Beige (MC); 2 (2, 3, 3, 3) skeins #4 Moorit.

Seven 7/16" buttons.

Gauge: 7 sts and 10 rows equal 1" over St st. Adjust needle sizes if necessary to obtain the correct gauge (see page 69).

Needle Suggestions: Size 3 for body and sleeves; size 2 for ribbing—straight and 16" circular.

BACK: With MC and smaller needles, CO 133 (141, 147, 155, 161) sts. Work k1, p1 rib for 1" ending on RS row. WS facing, purl across inc 8 sts evenly spaced: 141 (149, 155, 163, 169) sts. Work even until piece meas 10½ (11, 11, 11½, 11½)" from beg. BO 2 sts at beg of next 8 rows: 125 (133, 139, 147, 153) sts rem. Work even until piece meas 20½ (21½, 22, 23, 23½)" from beg. Divide sts onto 3 holders: 38 (42, 44, 47, 49) sts for each shoulder, and 49 (49, 51, 53, 55) sts for back neck.

RIGHT FRONT: With MC and smaller needles, CO 74 (78, 80, 84, 88) sts. Work k1, p1 rib for 1/2". With RS facing, rib 2 sts, work the One-Row Buttonhole (see page 74), rib to end. Work an addi-

"The Axes" pullover.

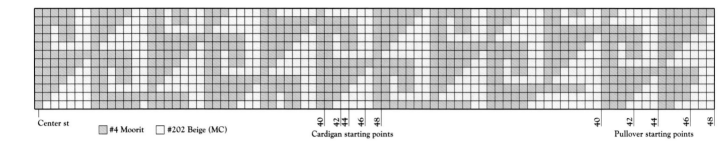

Center st · #4 Moorit □ #202 Beige (MC)

40 42 44 46 48
Cardigan starting points

40 42 44 46 48
Pullover starting points

CARDIGAN

Right Front: Beginning at center front, begin working graph at appropriate starting point. Work to center st. Work back to starting point.

Left Front: Beginning at side edge, begin working graph at appropriate starting point. Work to center st. Work back to starting point.

PULLOVER

Begin at appropriate starting point. Work to center st. Work back to starting point.

tional 1/2" of k1, p1 rib, ending on RS row. WS facing, purl across inc 4 sts evenly, maintain rib over last 7 sts: 78, (82, 84, 88, 92) sts. With RS facing, rib 7 sts and place on holder (Buttonhole Band): 71 (75, 77, 81, 85) sts rem. Change to larger needles and St st. Follow graph instructions. Work even until piece meas 10½ (11, 11, 11½, 11½)" from beg ending with a RS row. With WS facing, BO 2 sts at armhole edge 4 times: 63 (67, 69, 73, 77) sts rem. Work even until piece meas 18 (19, 19½, 20½, 21)" from beg ending with a WS row. **Shape neck:** At neck edge, keeping in pattern, BO 14 (14, 14, 15, 17) sts once, 4 sts once, 2 sts twice, then dec 1 st every other row 3 times: 38 (42, 44, 47, 49) sts rem. Keeping in pattern, work even until piece meas 20½ (21½, 22, 23, 23½)" from beg. Place rem shoulder sts on holder.

LEFT FRONT: Work as for Right Front reversing shaping and omitting buttonhole in bottom ribbing.

SLEEVES: With smaller needles and MC, CO 63 (67, 71, 75, 79) sts. Work k1, p1 rib for 1" ending on RS row. WS facing, purl across inc 7 (9, 11, 13, 15) sts evenly: 70 (76, 82, 88, 94) sts. Change to larger needles and St st. Inc 1 st each side every 4th row 30 (31, 31, 31, 31) times, then every 6th row 5 (5, 5, 6, 6) times: 140 (148, 154, 162, 168) sts. Work even until sleeve meas 17 (17½, 17½, 18, 18)" from beg. BO 2 sts at the beg of next 8 rows. Place rem 124 (132, 138, 146, 152) sts on holder.

BUTTON BANDS: Right: With smaller needles and MC, pick up the 7 sts of right Buttonhole Band from holder. *Work even in k1, p1 rib for approximately 2¾ (3, 3, 3¼, 3⅓)" from last buttonhole. With RS facing, rib 2 sts, work the One-Row Buttonhole (see page 74), rib to end. Rep from* 4 more times. Continue in k1, p1 rib for 2¼ (2½, 2½, 2¾, 2¾)". Do not break yarn. Place sts on holder. The last buttonhole will be made in the neckband. **Left:** Rep as for right Button Band, omitting buttonholes and breaking yarn.

FINISHING: BO fronts and back tog at shoulder seam (see page 75). With smaller needles, RS facing, and MC attached, rib 7 sts of right Buttonhole Band from holder, pick up and knit 35 (35, 37, 37, 39) sts along right neck edge, 49 (49, 51, 53, 55) sts from back holder, 35 (35, 37, 37, 39) sts along left neck edge, rib 7 sts of left Button Band from holder: 133 (133, 139, 141, 147) sts. Work k1, p1 rib for 1/2", work the One-Row Buttonhole at neckline on right front band. Work an additional 1/2" of k1, p1 rib. BO in pattern. Sew Button Bands to center front edges. BO sleeves onto the body (see page 75). Sew side and sleeve seams. Sew on buttons.

"The Red Palm" cap.

THE RED PALM

❦ *Designed by Kerstin Olsson* ❧

THE RED PALM
YOKE PULLOVER

Finished Size: 40 (44, 48)" approximate bust/chest width.

Materials: Kimmet Croft Fibers' Fairy Hare (60% Rambouillet wool, 40% Angora; 1 oz. = approx. 150 yards/137 meters): 8 (9, 10) oz. #FF103 (MC); 1/3 oz. each #FF102, #FF104, #FF106, #FF107, #FF108, and #FF95; 1/4 oz. #FF1 and #FF99.

Gauge: 7 sts and 10 rows equal 1" over St st. Adjust needle sizes if necessary to obtain the correct gauge (see page 69).

Needle Suggestions: Size 3 for unpatterned areas—16" and 29" circular, and double pointed; size 2 for patterned areas—16" and 29" circular, and double pointed; size 1 for ribbing—29" circular, and double pointed.

Note: Follow graph making increases or decreases in rounds indicated. This is necessary to make the sts in the round evenly divisible by the number of sts in the pattern repeat.

YOKE: (All sizes) With MC, waste yarn, smaller 16"needle, and using the Looping Provisional Cast On (see page 70), CO 120 sts. Place marker (pm) at beg of rnd. (The marker will be at the back of the right shoulder on the garment.) Join, being careful not to twist sts. With MC, work 2" in k1, p1 rib. (Later, the ribbing will be folded in half to the inside of the neckline, the waste yarn will be removed, and the live sts stitched in place. This allows for plenty of give in the neck.) K1 rnd MC, inc 24 sts evenly: 144 sts. Beg working from graph and change to 29" needle when necessary. When graph is complete, work in MC and inc 0 (4, 2) sts in first plain rnd: 378 (406, 434) sts. Change to larger needles. **Mark the Body and Sleeves:** Starting at the beg of the rnd, pm after: 116 (126, 136) sts for back, 73 (77, 81) sts for left sleeve, 116 (126, 136) sts for front, and 73 (77, 81) sts for right sleeve (4 markers in place). Break yarn. **Short Rows:** Short rows are worked to provide a better fit. They are basically used to lower the front neck and are worked back and forth in St st. Starting at beg of rnd (back of the right shoulder), sl sts of right sleeve, right front marker and 6 sts of right front to left-hand side of needle. With RS facing, join new yarn. Keeping tail at back of work, bring yarn from back to front between needle tips, sl first st on left-hand side of needle to right-hand side, yarn back (wrapped st). K5 sts of right front, sl marker, work to 5 sts beyond last marker (5 sts of left front worked). Continue with short rows: *Yarn forward; slip next st p-wise to right-hand needle. Yarn back; turn work. Slip first st back to right-hand needle (wrapped st). WS facing, purl to last marker (right front marker); slip marker, purl to the wrapped st, purl the wrap tog with the wrapped st on the needle, p5 more sts of right front; slip next st p-wise to right-hand needle. Yarn back; turn work. Slip first st back to right-hand needle. Yarn back (wrapped st). Knit to wrapped st of

left front. Knit the wrap tog with the wrapped st on the needle, then k5 more sts of left front. Rep from*. Work 5 sts further into the front sts of the sweater on each side 4 times total (40 sts = 8 short rows) ending at left front. Beg working circularly again until yoke at center front meas 8 (9, 10)" (measured straight up) or desired length from the beg of the color-work after the ribbing. End at back of the right shoulder marker.

DIVIDE SLEEVES AND BODY: Sleeves: With larger needles and Looping Provisional Cast On, CO 2 sets of 24 (28, 32) sts for the underarms and set aside. With larger 29" circular needle, knit across 116 (126, 136) back sts, drop yarn and needle. **Join new ball of yarn and larger 16" circular needle. Knit across 73 (77, 81) sts of left sleeve, then across cast-on sts placing marker after 12th (14th, 16th) st: 97 (105, 113) sts. Join and work even for a total of 20 rnds, ending at marker. Dec rnd: *K1, k2tog, work until 3 sts are left before marker, SSK, k1. Work 6 rnds even. Rep from* 16 (17, 18) more times: 63 (69, 75) sts. The sleeve is approximately 14½ (15¼, 16)" long. Change to dpn when necessary. Work 6 rnds even after last dec rnd. Final dec rnd: *K1, k2tog; rep from* 42 (46, 50) sts rem. Change to smaller dpn. Work k1, p1 rib for 2–3". BO in pattern. At left underarm, pick up larger 29" circular needle with yarn attached, remove the waste yarn from left underarm sts, knit up 24 (28, 32) sts; knit across 116 (126, 136) front sts, then drop yarn and needle. Rep from** for right sleeve. **Body:** At right underarm, pick up larger 29" circular nee-

dle with yarn attached, remove the waste yarn from right underarm sts, knit up 24 (28, 32) sts: 280 (308, 336) sts. Continue working in the rnd until desired length from neck rib less body rib length. Change to smaller dpn. Work k1, p1 rib for 2–3". BO in pattern.

FINISHING: Weave underarm seams. Sew in ends. Fold neck ribbing in half to inside. Remove waste yarn and stitch in place.

THE RED PALM YOKE CARDIGAN

Finished Size: 40 (44, 48)" approximate bust/chest width.

Materials: Kimmet Croft Fibers' Fairy Hare (60% Rambouillet wool, 40% Angora; 1 oz. = approx. 150 yards/137 meters): 8 (9, 10) oz. #FF103 (MC); 1/3 oz. each #FF102, #FF104, #FF106, #FF107, #FF108, and #FF95; 1/4 oz. #FF1 and #FF99.
Nine 5/8" buttons.

Gauge: 7 sts and 10 rows equal 1" over St st. Adjust needle sizes if necessary to obtain the correct gauge (see page 69).

Needle Suggestions: Size 3 for unpatterned areas—16" and 29" circular; size 2 for patterned areas—16" and 29" circular, and double pointed; size 1 for ribbing—29" circular, and double pointed.

Note: Follow graph making increases or decreases in rnds indicated. This is necessary in order to make the sts in the rnd evenly divisible by the number of sts in the pattern repeat.

CAP
Work even following graph.

JACKET
Work even following graph.

PULLOVER AND CARDIGAN
Rnd 13: inc 72 sts evenly: 216 sts.
Rnd 32: inc 72 (84, 108) sts evenly: 288 (300, 324) sts.
Rnd 47: inc 72 (102, 108) sts evenly: 360 (402, 432) sts.
Rnd 63: inc 18 (0, 0) sts evenly: 378 (402, 432) sts.

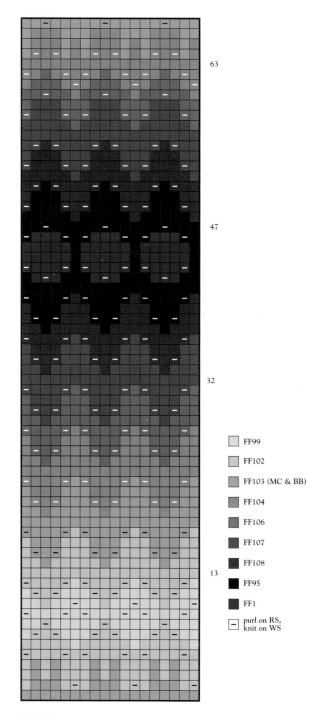

FF99

FF102

FF103 (MC & BB)

FF104

FF106

FF107

FF108

FF95

FF1

purl on RS,
knit on WS

YOKE: (All Sizes) With MC and rib needle, CO 121 sts. Work back and forth in k1, p1 rib for 1/2". With RS facing, rib 3 sts, work the One-Row Buttonhole (see page 74), rib to end. Work k1, p1 rib for 1/2", ending on RS row. With WS facing, work 8 rib sts and place on holder (left Button Band), purl 105 sts, at the same time inc 39 sts evenly, rib rem 8 sts. With RS facing, rib 8 sts and place on holder (right Buttonhole Band): 144 sts rem. Place marker (pm) at beg of rnd. (The marker will be at the center front of the garment.) Join, being careful not to twist sts. With MC, k2 rnds. Beg working from graph and change to 29" needles when necessary. When graph is complete, work in MC and inc 0 (4, 2) sts in first plain rnd: 378 (406, 434) sts. **Mark the Body and Sleeves:** Starting at the beg of the rnd, pm after: 58 (63, 68) sts for right front, 73 (77, 81) sts for right sleeve, 116 (126, 136) sts for back, and 73 (77, 81) sts for left sleeve. Work rem 58 (63, 68) sts for left front (4 markers in place). **Short Rows:** Short rows are worked to provide a better fit. They are basically used to lower the front neck and are worked back and forth in St st. Starting at beg of rnd, work to last marker (left sleeve marker); slip marker. Work 5 sts of left front. *Yarn forward; slip next st p-wise to right-hand needle. Yarn back, turn work. Slip first st back to right-hand needle (wrapped st). WS facing, purl to last marker (right sleeve marker); slip marker. P5 sts of right front; slip next st p-wise to right-hand needle. Yarn back; turn work. Slip first st back to right-hand nee-

dle. Yarn back (wrapped st). Knit to wrapped st of left front sts. Knit the wrap tog with the wrapped st, then k5 more sts of left front. Rep from*. Work 5 sts further into the front sts of the sweater on each side 4 times total (40 sts = 8 short rows). Beg working circularly again until yoke at center front meas 8 (9, 10)" or desired length from beg of colorwork.

DIVIDE SLEEVES AND BODY: Sleeves: With larger needles and Looping Provisional Cast On, CO 2 sets of 24 (28, 32) sts for the underarms and set aside. With larger 29" circular needle, knit across 58 (63, 68) sts of right front, drop yarn and needle. **Join new ball of yarn and larger 16" circular needle. Knit across 73 (77, 81) sts of right sleeve, then across cast-on sts placing marker after 12th (14th, 16th) st: 97 (105, 113) sts. Join and work even for a total of 20 rnds, ending at marker. Dec rnd: *K1, k2tog, work until 3 sts are left before marker, SSK, k1. Work 6 rnds even. Rep from* 16 (17, 18) more times: 63 (69, 75) sts. The sleeve is approximately 14½ (15¼, 16)" long. Change to dpn when necessary. Work 6 rnds even after last dec rnd. Final dec rnd: *K1, k2tog; rep from*: 42 (46, 50) sts. Change to smaller dpn. Work k1, p1 rib for 2–3". BO in pattern. At right underarm, pick up larger 29" circular needle with yarn attached, remove the waste yarn from right underarm sts, knit up 24 (28, 32) sts; knit across 116 (126, 136) back sts, then drop yarn and needle. Rep from** for left sleeve. **Body:** At left underarm, pick up larger 29" circular needle with yarn attached, remove the waste

yarn from left underarm sts, knit up 24 (28, 32) sts; knit across rem 58 (63, 68) sts of left front: 280 (308, 336) sts. Continue working in the rnd until piece meas 14 (15, 16)" from underarm or desired length. BO 4 sts at center front. Baste down center front of sweater. Machine stitch twice on each side. Cut open.

BUTTONHOLE BAND: Beg at top of right front, using MC and rib needles, pick up the 8 sts of right Buttonhole Band from holder. *Work even in k1, p1 rib for approximately 3 (3¼, 3½)" from last buttonhole. With WS facing, rib 3 sts, work the One-Row Buttonhole (see page 74), rib to end. Rep from * 6 more times. Continue in k1, p1 rib for 1½ (1¾, 2)". Break yarn. Place sts on holder. The last buttonhole will be made in the bottom ribbing.

BUTTON BAND: Rep as for Buttonhole Band, omitting buttonholes, and do not break yarn.

BOTTOM RIBBING: With rib needle and RS facing, pick up sts from left Button Band (make sure band is not twisted), body sts from waste yarn, and right Button Band sts (make sure band is not twisted). With MC attached at left Button Band, work back and forth in k1, p1 rib for 1½", end with RS. With WS facing, rib 3 sts, work the One-Row Buttonhole, rib to end. Work 1/2" of k1, p1 rib. BO in pattern.

FINISHING: Weave underarm seams. Sew button and Buttonhole Bands to center fronts. Sew in ends. Sew on buttons.

Finished Size: 40 (44, 48)" approximate bust/chest width.

Materials: Kimmet Croft Fibers' Fairy Hare (60% Rambouillet wool, 40% Angora; 1 oz. = approx. 150 yards/137 meters): 8 (9, 10) oz. #FF103 (MC and BB); 1 oz. #FF1; 2/3 oz. each #FF102, #FF104, #FF106, #FF107, #FF108, and #FF95; 1/2 oz. #FF99.

Nine 7/16" buttons.

Gauge: 7 sts and 10 rows equal 1" over St st. Adjust needle sizes if necessary to obtain the correct gauge (see page 69).

Needle Suggestions: Size 3 for unpatterned areas; size 2 for patterned areas; size 1 for bands.

RIGHT FRONT: With smallest needle and BB(band color), CO 154 (161, 168) sts. K6 rows. K16 sts, *work the One-Row Buttonhole (see page 74), k17 (18, 19) sts, rep from* 6 times total; work the One-Row Buttonhole, k15 (16, 17) sts. K5 rows (total of 6 garter st ridges). Change to medium needles and work 2 rows St st in BB color. Begin working from graph. Work even for 1½ (2, 2½)". Keeping in pattern, inc 1 st at neck edge (right side) 4 times, inc 2 sts once, inc 3 sts once, inc 5 sts once, inc 7 sts once: 175 (182, 189) sts. After completing graph work even in MC until piece meas approximately 5¾ (6¼, 6¾)" from beg. RS facing, BO 62 (69, 76) sts for armhole. Work 2 rows. RS facing, BO 2 sts at armhole edge 4 times: 105 sts rem (all sizes). This is the side seam and should meas approximately 15". Work even for 1". Piece should measure approximately 10½ (11, 11½)" from beg. BO rem 105 sts. With smallest needles and BB, pick up and k80 (85, 90) sts along bottom edge. K7 more rows. Next row: K74 (79, 84) sts, work One-Row Buttonhole, knit to end of row. K6 more rows. Using medium needle, BO on reverse side of knit (8 garter ridges).

LEFT FRONT: Work same as Right Front, reversing the shaping and omitting buttonholes.

BACK: With largest needle and MC, CO 142 (156, 170) sts. Change to smallest needle. Work 1" in garter st. Change to largest needle and work even in St st until piece meas 16" from beg. BO 2 sts at the beg of next 8 rows. Work even until piece meas 26 (27, 28)" from beg. Place rem sts on 3 holders: 40 (44, 48) sts for each shoulder, and 46 (52, 58) sts for back.

SLEEVES: With largest needle and MC, CO 62 (70, 80) sts. Change to smallest needle. Work 1" in garter st. Change to largest needle and St st, inc 6 (10, 12) sts evenly across next row: 68 (80, 92) sts. Inc 1 st each side every 4th row 31 (31, 32) times and every 6th row 5 (6, 6) times: 140 (154, 168) sts. Work even until piece meas 17½ (18, 18½)" from beg. BO 2 sts beg of next 8 rows. Place rem sts on holder.

FINISHING: Join shoulder seams. With smallest needle and BB, pick up and k45 (48, 50) sts from right center front to shoulder seam, 46 (52, 58) sts from back neck holder, 45 (48, 50) sts from shoulder seam to left center front: 136 (148, 158) sts. K3 more rows (2 garter ridges). On the next row dec 13 (16, 18) sts evenly across row. K1 more row. On next row, k3, work One-Row Buttonhole, knit to end of row. K1 more row. On next row dec 6 (9, 11) sts evenly across row: 117 (123, 129) sts. K3 more rows. Using medium needle, BO on reverse side in knit. BO or sew sleeves into armhole (see page 75). Sew side and sleeve seams.

THE RED PALM CAP

Finished Size: 21 (23)" circumference.

Materials: Kimmet Croft Fibers' Fairy Hare (60% Rambouillet wool, 40% Angora; 1 oz. = approx. 150 yards/137 meters.): 1/2 oz. #FF103 (MC); 1/4 oz. each #FF99, #FF102, #FF104, #FF106, #FF107, #FF108, #FF95, and #FF1.

Gauge: 7 sts and 10 rows equal 1" over St st. Adjust needle sizes if necessary to obtain the correct gauge (see page 69).

Needle Suggestions: Size 2 for patterned area—16" circular, and double pointed; size 1 for ribbing—16"circular.

With MC and smaller needle, CO 136 (146) sts. Place marker at beg of rnd. Join, being careful not to twist sts. Work 3/4" in k1, p1 rib. Change to larger needle, work 1 rnd, inc 14 (16) sts evenly: 150 (162) sts. Work even following graph. After completing graph, work even in MC until piece meas approximately 7" from beg. With MC, work 1 rnd, dec 3 (1) sts evenly in rnd: 147 (161) sts. **Seven Point Crown:** Begin working with circular needle and change to dpn when necessary. Work dbl dec at seven points as follows: sl 2 sts k-wise tog, k1, p2sso. *Rnd 1:* *K18 (20), dbl dec; rep from* 6 times. *Rnd 2 and even numbered rnds:* Knit.

Rnd 3: *K16 (18), dbl dec; rep from* 6 times. Continue in this manner, working 1 less st before and after each dbl dec until 21 sts rem. Work dbl dec around: 7 sts rem. Draw yarn through 7 sts. Sew in ends.

THE LATE AUTUMN

✄ *Designed by* *Annika Malmström-Bladini* ✄

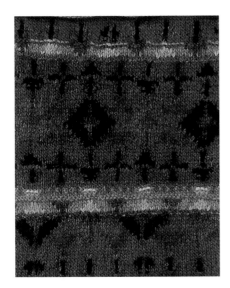

THE LATE AUTUMN
YOKE PULLOVER

Finished Size: 40 (44, 48)" approximate bust/chest width.

Materials: Kimmet Croft Fibers' Fairy Hare (60% Rambouillet wool, 40% Angora; 1 oz. = approx. 150 yards/137 meters): 8 (9, 10) oz. #FF1 (MC); 1 oz. #FF70; 1/2 oz each #FF87, and #FF88; 1/4 oz. each #FF90, #FF93, #FF73, #FF89, and #FF80.

Gauge: 7 sts and 10 rows equal 1" over St st. Adjust needle sizes if necessary to obtain the correct gauge (see page 69).

Needle Suggestions: Size 3 for unpatterned areas—16" and 29" circular, and double pointed; size 2 for patterned areas—16" and 29" circular, and double pointed; size 1 for ribbing—29" circular, and double pointed.

Note: Follow graph making increases or decreases in rounds indicated. This is necessary to make the sts in the round evenly divisible by the number of sts in the pattern repeat.

YOKE: (All sizes) With MC, waste yarn, smaller 16" needle, and using the Looping Provisional Cast On (see page 70), CO 120 sts. Place marker (pm) at beg of rnd. (The marker will be at the back of the right shoulder on the garment.) Join, being careful not to twist sts. With MC, work 2" in k1, p1 rib. (Later, the ribbing will be folded in half to the inside of the neckline, the waste yarn removed and the live sts stitched in place. This allows for plenty of give in the neck.) K1 rnd MC, inc 20 sts evenly: 140 sts. Beg working from graph and change to 29" needle when necessary. When graph is complete, work in MC: 378 (406, 434) sts. Change to larger needles. **Mark the Body and Sleeves:** Starting at the beg of the rnd, pm after: 116 (126, 136) sts for back, 73 (77, 81) sts for left sleeve, 116 (126, 136) sts for front, and 73 (77, 81) sts for right sleeve (4 markers in place). Break yarn. **Short Rows:** Short rows are worked to provide a better fit. They are basically used

to lower the front neck and are worked back and forth in St st. Starting at beg of rnd (back of the right shoulder), sl sts of right sleeve, right front marker and 6 sts of right front to left-hand side of needle. With RS facing, join new yarn. Keeping tail at back of work, bring yarn from back to front between needle tips, sl first st on left-hand side of needle to right-hand side, yarn back (wrapped st). K5 sts of right front, sl marker, work to 5 sts beyond last marker (5 sts of left front worked). Continue with short rows: *Yarn forward; slip next st p-wise to right-hand needle. Yarn back; turn work. Slip first st back to right-hand needle (wrapped st). WS facing, purl to last marker (right front marker); slip marker, purl to the wrapped st, purl the wrap tog with the wrapped st on the needle, p5 more sts of right front; slip next st p-wise to right-hand needle. Yarn back; turn work. Slip first st back to right-hand needle. Yarn back (wrapped st). Knit to wrapped st of left front. Knit the wrap tog with the wrapped st on the needle, then k5 more sts of left front. Rep from*. Work 5 sts further into the front sts of the sweater on each side 4 times total (40 sts = 8 short rows) ending at left front. Beg working circularly again until yoke at center front meas 8 (9, 10)" (measured straight up) or desired length from the beg of the colorwork after the ribbing. End at back of the right shoulder marker.

DIVIDE SLEEVES AND BODY: Sleeves: With larger needles and Looping Provisional Cast On, CO 2 sets of 24 (28, 32) sts for the underarms and set aside. With larger 29" circular needle, knit across 116 (126, 136) back sts, drop yarn

CAP

Work entire graph even in pattern repeat as given.

PULLOVER

Rnd 10: inc 84 sts: 224 sts.

Rnd 29: inc 84 (112, 112) sts: 308 (336, 336) sts.

Rnd 37: inc 56 (56, 70) sts: 364 (392, 406) sts.

Rnd 40: inc 14 (14, 28) sts: 378 (406, 434) sts.

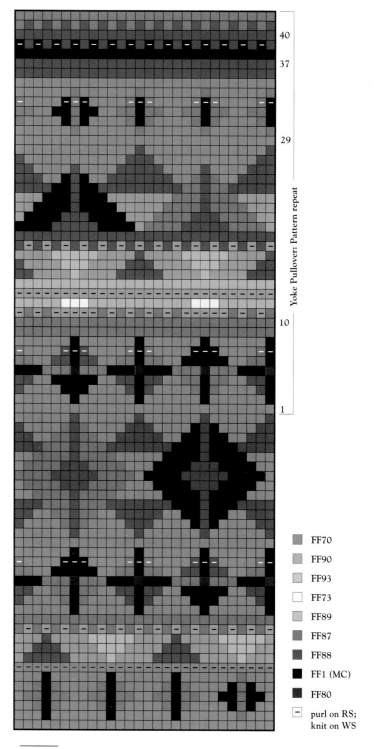

Yoke Pullover: Pattern repeat

▨	FF70
▨	FF90
☐	FF93
☐	FF73
▨	FF89
▨	FF87
▨	FF88
■	FF1 (MC)
■	FF80
−	purl on RS; knit on WS

and needle. **Join new ball of yarn and larger 16" circular needle. Knit across 73 (77, 81) sts of left sleeve, then across cast-on sts placing marker after 12th (14th, 16th) st: 97 (105, 113) sts. Join and work even for a total of 20 rnds, ending at marker. Dec rnd: *K1, k2tog, work until 3 sts are left before marker, SSK, k1. Work 6 rnds even. Rep from* 16 (17, 18) more times: 63 (69, 75) sts rem. The sleeve is approximately 14½ (15¼, 16)" long. Change to dpn when necessary. Work 6 rnds even after last dec rnd. Final dec rnd: *K1, k2tog; rep from*: 42 (46, 50) sts rem. Change to smaller dpn. Work k1, p1 rib for 2–3". BO in pattern. At left underarm, pick up larger 29" circular needle with yarn attached, remove the waste yarn from left underarm sts, knit up 24 (28, 32) sts; knit across 116 (126, 136) front sts, then drop yarn and needle. Rep from** for right sleeve. **Body:** At right underarm, pick up larger 29" circular needle with yarn attached, remove the waste yarn from right underarm sts, knit up 24 (28, 32) sts: 280 (308, 336) sts. Continue working in the rnd until desired length from neck rib less body rib length. Change to smaller dpn. Work in k1, p1 rib for 2–3". BO in pattern.

FINISHING: Weave underarm seams. Sew in ends. Turn neck ribbing in half to inside. Remove waste yarn and st in place.

Finished Size: 23" circumference.

Materials: Kimmet Croft Fibers' Fairy Hare (60% Rambouillet wool, 40% Angora; 1 oz. = approx. 150 yards/137 meters): 1 oz. #FF1 (MC), and #FF70; 1/2 oz. #FF87, and #FF88; 1/4 oz. #FF90, #FF93, #FF73, #FF89, and #FF80.

Gauge: 7 sts and 10 rows equal 1" over St st. Adjust needle sizes if necessary to obtain the correct gauge (see page 69).

Needle Suggestions: Size 2 for patterned area—16" circular, and double pointed; size 1 for ribbing—16" circular.

With MC and smaller needle, CO 146. Place marker at beg of rnd. Join, being careful not to twist sts. Work 3/4" in k1, p1 rib. Change to larger needle, work 1 rnd, inc 22 sts evenly: 168 sts. Work even following graph. After completing graph, work even in MC until piece meas approximately 7" from beg. With MC, work 1 rnd, dec 7 sts evenly: 161 sts. **Seven Point Crown:** Begin working with circular needle and change to dpn when necessary. Work dbl dec at seven points as follows: sl 2 sts k-wise tog, k1, p2sso. *Rnd 1:* *K20, dbl dec; rep from* 6 more times. *Rnd 2 and all even numbered rnds:* Knit. *Rnd 3:* *K18, dbl dec; rep from* 6 more times. Continue in this manner, working 1 less st before and after each dbl dec until 21 sts rem. Work dbl dec around: 7 sts rem. Draw yarn through 7 sts. Sew in ends.

RESOURCES

BIBLIOGRAPHY

Häglund, Ulla with Ingrid
Mesterton. *Bohus Stickning*. Göteborg: Bokforlaget Atlantis, 1980.
This Swedish book is out of print.
Norbury, James and Margaret Agutter. *Odham's Encyclopedia of Knitting*. Long Acre, London:
Odhams Books Limited, no date.
Stanley, Montse. *The Handknitter's Handbook*. New York: Sterling
Publishing Co., 1986.
Walker, Barbara G. *A Second Treasury of Knitting Patterns*.
Charles Scribner's Sons, 1970.

*Bohus Stickning documents are
available from The Women's Archives
at The Gothenburg University.*

SWEDISH MUSEUMS HOUSING BOHUS STICKNING COLLECTIONS

The Röhss Arts & Crafts Museum
Röhsska Konstslöjdmuseet
Box 53178
S-400 15 Göteborg
Sweden

The City of Gothenburg Museum
Göteborgs Stadsmuseum
Norra Hamngatan 12-14
S-411 14 Göteborg
Sweden

Bohusläns Museum
Box 33
S-451 15 Uddevalla
Sweden

YARN SOURCES

"Fairy Hare" angora-blend yarn:
Kimmet Croft Fibers
5850 Schudy Road
Wisconsin Rapids, WI 54495
(715) 421-0121
*Exclusive manufacturer and supplier of
"Fairy Hare" yarn for designs featured in
this book. Yarn available in open stock or in
kits.*

*Alice Starmore's "Campion" by Broad
Bay Company:*
Yarns International
Westwood Center II
5110 Ridgefield Road
at River Road
Bethesda, MD 20816
(800) 927-6728

Tomato Factory Yarn Company
8 Church Street
Lambertville, NJ 08530
(800) 483-7959

Jamieson and Smith Shetland Yarn:
Schoolhouse Press
6899 Cary Bluff Road
Pittsville, WI 54466
(800) 968-5648 (YOU-KNIT)

INDEX